Journey

to the

LAND OF THE FLIES

&

OTHER TRAVELS

Journey to the
LAND OF THE FLIES

Other Travels

ALDO BUZZI

translated from the Italian
by Ann Goldstein

RANDOM HOUSE NEW YORK

Library of Congress Cataloging-in-Publication information is available.
ISBN 0-679-44810-1

Manufactured in the United States of America on acid-free paper
24689753
First Edition

Book design by Lilly Langotsky

A painter in Ubeda; who, when asked what he was painting, said: "What comes out."

CERVANTES, *DON QUIXOTE*

Collected here, in one volume, are two books originally published in Italy by Scheiwiller. The contents have been reviewed, corrected, lengthened, shortened (especially "Travels"), and also disassembled and reassembled in a different way, and have now, I hope, finally reached their proper form.

Contents

JOURNEY
to the
LAND OF THE FLIES
&
OTHER TRAVELS

Chekhov in Sondrio

I have enlarged some early Russian postcards, and looking at them one enters into that world, just before our birth—a most attractive and comprehensible time, with people in uniform, soldiers, students, civil servants, dogs, horses, a tearoom, a printer's on the second floor, a man in a long overcoat walking with hands clasped behind him.

—Letter to the author from Saul Steinberg

I

In Milan many years ago, among the trees of our "Summer Garden," there was a Russian *isba* (a log house). I remember the great logs of dark wood, the veranda, where an old maidservant (perhaps I am getting this mixed up with Gogol) welcomed guests with a deep bow. It was not far from the zoo, where a Siberian wolf paced continually from one corner to the other of its cage, hoping obstinately to find a hole through which to go out into the steppe of Milan. A crow landed on the meadow and, as Chekhov says, "before planting itself on its feet, leaped a few times. . . ."

The *isba* is no longer there. The proprietor, Paolin (Pasenka)—may God grant him eternal peace—is no longer there, either. The nephew of Pasenka, having succeeded his uncle, demolished the *russkaya isba*—the wood had rotted—and built in its place a kiosk lacking any Russian character and, in general, any character at all.

"Vodka," said Bulgakov's Professor Filip Filipovich Preobrazhenski—who succeeded in transforming a mongrel dog into a proletarian by transplanting into him the pituitary gland of a strolling balalaika player— "must be ninety proof, not eighty." On his antipasto table (which, according to Russian custom, precedes the lunch table), in spite of the restrictions of the moment (the NEP), there were always three different bottles of vodka. He was one of those who "can distinguish, with their eyes blindfolded, the vodka of Koshelyov from Smirnov No. 21."

I leaned on the bar of the kiosk. "A Georgian vodka, *batiushka*."

Georgian vodka is the vodka of Stalin; it cuts off your legs and makes you feel sparks bursting from your stomach through your whole body.

The nephew of Pasenka "looked at me obliquely, like a wolf."

"We have no vodka, High Nobility."

On the path behind me an unorthodox troika (drawn by a single shaggy pony), crowded with frightened children and driven by a citified muzhik, was speeding slowly among the local collegiate registrars. There appeared in the cloudy sky a flock of cranes in the form of a triangle, guided by a leader who cried out his orders in a loud voice.

"Then, brother, if you don't have vodka give me a Coke. Better a tomtit in hand than a crane in the sky."

The cranes were already distant, and because of the wind the triangle was turning into a circle. When cranes descend to rest, they set sentinels to watch over the sleeping flock, and these stand upright on only one leg, holding on their raised foot a stone, so that if sleep strikes, the stone will fall to the ground and the noise will wake them. . . . Is it possible, I thought, that someone would eat them?

II

Lenin died on January 21, 1924. In six days a provisional wooden mausoleum was built in Red Square to hold the embalmed corpse. On the twenty-sixth it was decided to give Lenin's name to Petrograd. The mausoleum was remade, again of wood, in May. Joseph Roth saw it in 1926: "It is a mixture, unintended but symbolically effective, of a monument and a speaker's platform." That description also goes for the permanent monument of red granite, constructed in the years 1929–30 and designed by the architect Aleksei Shchusev, who was the author of the two temporary mausoleums as well. Shchusev perhaps had in mind the Kaaba, the gray cube in the courtyard of the Great Mosque at Mecca, around which Muslim pilgrims walk seven times. At Lenin's tomb the pilgrims form a long line—an example of the innumerable lines that are seen everywhere. During the war Lenin was evacuated to Kuibyshev, the ancient Samara, then had to cohabit with

Stalin. Now everything is as it was before. When Ho Chi Minh (He Who Illuminates) died in Hanoi, they embalmed him like Lenin and built him a mausoleum imitating Shchusev's. To finish up they named Saigon Ho Chi Minh City. Another imitation of Lenin's tomb is in Ulan Bator, the capital of Mongolia, "where even the butterflies sting" (Shklovsky).

Shchusev studied architecture in Paris. In the center of Moscow, in the years 1931–35, he built the Moscow Hotel—of red granite and white marble, fourteen stories high, enlarged in '70—in the place where, until 1913, the city's biggest market for meat, chicken, fish, game, vegetables had been; one of the marvels of Moscow, it was demolished like Les Halles in Paris, probably for the same reasons.

One of the systems adopted to reduce the lines in front of the stores is reported by Leonid Abalkin, a corresponding member of the Academy of Sciences of the U.S.S.R. "Take, for example, sausages," writes the academician. "There is the usual kind that costs 2 rubles a kilo, and there is the higher-quality kind at 4.50 rubles a kilo. In front of the stores that sell these sausages there were always long lines. We doubled the price (to 9 rubles a kilo) and the situation totally changed."

This method of solving problems is as ancient in Russia as the use of the abacus. Chekhov made a long journey to the island of Sakhalin, at the far end of Eastern Siberia, to visit the penitentiaries there. A *katorga* (prison) official said to him, "The prisoners, especially those in chains, love to present every sort of stupid petition. When I was appointed here and toured the prison for the first time, I received fifty petitions; I accepted them and announced that only those prisoners whose petitions were not worthy of attention would be punished. Only two petitions were in order; the others were mere nonsense, and therefore I ordered a sound flogging to be given to forty-eight individuals. The next time, twenty-five petitions were presented, then fewer, and then even fewer. Now they present me with no more petitions."

Chekhov made this journey in 1890, over a hundred years ago, at the age of thirty. Already ill since '84, he must have dealt with discomforts and fatigues of every kind.

He left Moscow April 21st,

went from Moscow to Yaroslavl by train,

Yaroslavl–Perm by boat on the Volga and the Kama,

Perm–Tyumen by train,

Tyumen–Sretensk by coach, crossing Lake Baikal in a boat (about three thousand kilometers),

Sretensk–Nikolayevsk by boat on the Shilka and the Amur,

Nikolayevsk–Sakhalin by ship,

arriving at Aleksandrovsk (Sakhalin) the eleventh of July.

The day before, a prisoner had been whipped. "He showed me his buttocks, livid with bruises. . . ." Eastern Siberia was inhabited by clean people. "At night when you enter the room where they sleep, there is neither a stink nor the 'odor of Russians.' . . . A cleanliness that our Ukrainians do not even dream of, and so they are infinitely cleaner than Russians. . . . The bread is most delicious."

The bread in the Siberia of Dostoyevsky, closer to Moscow, was also very good. "The climate is excellent," one reads at the beginning of *The House of the Dead*. "The girls there flower like roses. . . . The game runs through the streets and throws itself in the way of the hunter. There one drinks champagne in inordinate quantities. The caviar is marvelous. . . . Altogether, it is a blessed land." For anyone who was outside the prisons.

Escape was not so difficult. Trotsky fled from the village where he was confined, on a sled drawn by three reindeer. "Like Santa Claus," said Nabokov.

☞

There are some similarities between the United States and Russia. In 1861, Czar Alexander II abolished serfdom. Two years later, in 1863, Abraham Lincoln abolished slavery. Both nations are ignorant of the bidet and rightly consider the ground floor of a building to be the first floor. (Thus, what we Italians call the first floor is for them the second, which causes continual errors in translations from the two languages.) Other similarities: a ban on selling alcohol near a church; the importance of firefighters, given the frequency of fires ("As everyone knows," says Turgenev, "our provincial towns burn down every five years"); finally, both Americans and Russians build in the country little wooden houses in a neoclassical style. Both love picnics and stuffed turkey, and both have a generic name for cats: the Americans Pussycat, the Russians Vaska, the diminutive of Vasily (Basil), the blessed one of Red Square.

One more thing the United States of America and the Union of Soviet Socialist Republics had in common:

their names—artificial, bureaucratic, too long, and, therefore, often replaced by two (similar) sets of initials, U.S.A. and U.S.S.R., difficult to pronounce, or by two abbreviations, United States and Soviet Union, or simply by the dear old names, America and Russia. Now some Russians call their country Absurdistan.

Differences: paper money. In the U.S.A. bills are green and all of the same size, which is not very practical; and in the U.S.S.R., or, rather, in Russia, they are of different colors, like Easter eggs: orange for one-ruble bills, green for threes, azure for fives, pink for tens, gray for fifties, and rainbow for hundreds. Mayakovsky says:

And you who, through work and melancholy, have a face crumpled and green like a three-ruble bill.

The differences are not limited to bills.

⌒

Petersburg, old names: the Liteyny Prospect is one of the few streets whose old names were preserved. At No. 27 Pestel Ulitsa, in a big Moorish-style mansion at the corner of Liteyny Prospect, lived Joseph Brodsky.

Pestel is the name of the leader of the Decembrists who was hanged, with four others, in 1826. Officers' Street, where Tolstoy lived when he left Turgenev's house; Four Corners Street; Christmas Street; Karavannaya Ulitsa (Caravan Street), where the caravans bringing tea from China arrived; the Sennaya (Haymarket Square); Chain Bridge; Kalinkin Bridge, where the ghost of Akaky Akakyevich appeared, in search of his stolen overcoat.

The Millionnaya—Millions Street, like Miami's Millionaires' Row—which today is called Khalturin Ulitsa, was the home of the English Club. It was the most exclusive club for the aristocracy, and memorable banquets were held there. In Moscow, too, there was an English Club: servants in livery, in wigs and silk stockings. After a toast, glasses were thrown to the ground. Feoktist was the most famous chef at the English Club in Moscow at the beginning of the nineteenth century. Cooks often had strange names. Prince Bolkonsky's father's cook was called Foka, a Byzantine name; Tit was Kutuzov's old cook, harassed by the servants; Taras was the very skillful cook of Count Rostov, who not for nothing paid him a thousand rubles. ("What a sauté of woodcock in Madeira we'll have, *ma chère!*")

In restaurants the waiters were Tartars.

The Russians say Tatàrs, but, according to the critic Giampaolo Dossena, "one ends up calling them Tartars, because they are frightening: an allusion to Tartarus, the classical name of Hell." They had lost their former fierceness and become obliging. Tartar waiter, in tails and flourishing a napkin, to Stepan Arkadyevich Oblonsky, the brother of Anna Karenina: "Your usual cheese?" Oblonsky: "Yes, Parmesan."

Some memories of the ancient atrocities remained. People said, "An uninvited guest is worse than a Tartar." "Traveling," wrote Mandelstam, "I would read Zoshchenko's best book and be happy as a Tatàr who has stolen a hundred rubles."

Their contribution to Russian (and international) cuisine: tartar sauce (it's impossible to say "tatàr" sauce) and steak tartare.

Music was entrusted to the Gypsies. The men played and sang, the women danced and sang and at the end circled around the tables with a tray of champagne glasses, on which the clientele, after being served, left their offerings. Some of the Gypsy women were very beautiful, and might be bought by a rich patron: Sergei Nikolayevich, Tolstoy's brother, who had a horror of flies and gnats, bought one and married her. She was a good wife.

☞

"Moscow of white stone" (Pushkin), "mother of cities" (Chekhov), "market of the fiancées" (Pushkin), "Moscow the drunkard" (Esenin).

Old names: Street of the Hurried, Sparrow Hill, Robbers' Street, Old Woodcutters' Street, Guardians of Hunting Dogs Street, Gazette Street, Cooks' Street, Bakers' Street, Knives Street, Pump Square, where the bird market was.

The Boloto (the swamp) was the great square where, in 1775, the Cossack Emelyan Pugachov, the leader of the terrible revolt of the serfs and Cossacks, was beheaded. After the execution the body was cut in pieces, and the pieces were set out in various quarters of the city.

Another Cossack, Stenka Razin, who, before Pugachov, had led a similar revolt, was beheaded in Moscow (1671) in the place reserved for executions—that is, the round stone platform (Lobnoye Mesto) in Red Square beside the Cathedral of Blessed Basil—and to him is dedicated the street that goes past the gigantic Rossiya (Russia) Hotel, near Red Square, whose construction caused a good piece of old Moscow to be thoughtlessly destroyed. It is the street, frequented by crows, that the tourist—barely settled in one of the hotel's thirty-two hundred rooms, and having taken a quick look at Millet's gleaners, hung on the wall with a big rusty nail—hurries along, eager for his first look at the magical apparition of the gold domes of the Kremlin.

Cossack names: Ostap, Kozolup, Doloto, Kirdyaga, Taras, Kasyan, Kolopyor, Pidsytok, Zakrutyguba.

Cossack proverb: "Endure, Cossack, and you will become *ataman* [chieftain]."

Cossack war cry: "Ghik, ghik!"—quite similar to the cry of the crow.

Crows appear in the first Russian literary document: "Song of the Campaign of Igor." According to Hesiod, they live nine times as long as man, and ravens even longer. "Crows, numberless as flies," says Gogol. They are everywhere: on city sidewalks, in gardens, in the yellow fields of rye, in the sky, in the forests.

> For the third day rain falls
> gnaws the gray ice
> and of the crow on the birch tree
> washes the beak.
>
> (Tarkovsky)

In spite of being a kind of hyena, in spite of its funereal color, and in spite of Turgenev's calling it "the most respectable bird, known for its devotion to its family," the crow has in itself something of the ridiculous. The word "crow" is used as an insult, a synonym for "lazybones," "idler": "Why did you stop, crow?"

⌒

Russians as I imagined them from novels and from translations: red-haired, like almost all the characters of Chekhov and Dostoyevsky (even the cows in the fields have red coats). Usually consumptive. They often clear their throats. They bow low to the ground. They call each other *batiushka* (little father), *matushka* (little mother), little dove, brother, benefactor, High Nobility. They stamp their feet on the ground, like horses, when they are angry. They spit on the ground as a sign of disdain. They live, in general, on the fourth floor (the fourth floor of the translator, which is usually the third floor for us Italians, or French or Germans). They walk not up and down but from one corner to another.

The Great Russians (of the north) have red hair, sky-blue eyes, and "noses in the shape of an onion," like Tolstoy—he says it himself, in a letter. The Little

Russians (of the south), like Gogol and Chekhov, have dark eyes and black hair——cut, at one time, in such a way that they were nicknamed "tufts." The barber left a kind of mane in the center of the skull, while the two sides were shaved. In Rome the movie makeup people called this haircut "Bashkir style." The custom had already been lost by Chekhov's time, I think; but in prison a convict still had half his head completely shaved, so that if he escaped he would be easily recognizable.

The women?

"In Russia," says Gogol, "everything loves to present itself in grand proportions, everything without exception: mountains, and forests, and steppes, and faces, and lips, and feet." Like the Bobolina, also described by Gogol: "one of whose legs alone appeared bigger than the entire torso of one of those dandies who fill the salons nowadays."

"Russia of the heavy buttocks," says Blok.

"I love their little feet," Pushkin says, "but you probably wouldn't find, in all Russia, three pairs of women's feet that are well made."

And there is the marvelous Natasha of *War and Peace*.

☙

Consumption was the national disease. It was not believed to be contagious; the sick and the healthy lived together. The cure was to go to the Crimea to drink koumiss—fermented mare's milk—once drunk by the ancient Scythians. Tolstoy and Chekhov cured themselves this way.

Two of Tolstoy's brothers died of consumption. Also Dostoyevsky's mother and his first wife. Dostoyevsky himself died from coughing blood. He died on a sofa, an item of furniture very often used by the Russians for sleeping (following a custom that had come from the Orient) and for dying. Even Stalin, according to Molotov, died on a sofa. People often slept without undressing, as the muzhiks habitually did, at times not even taking off their boots or their *lapty* (clogs). The typical sofa was covered with oilcloth.

Sleeping was not a problem. Tolstoy, who was born on a sofa, made himself an overcoat of rough canvas, which he put on when he wanted to spend the night under a tree in his garden at Yasnaya Polyana. For a pillow he used a big dictionary. And Mandelstam tells of an amputee who at night took off his wooden leg and used it for a pillow.

It was a common custom to have one's heels scratched by the servants, in order to sleep better. The servants themselves slept almost anywhere except on a bed or a sofa; usually it was on the ground, with a newspaper for a mattress, or on the big Russian stove.

The younger daughter of Tolstoy, Alexandra (Sasha), also went to the Crimea to be treated by drinking koumiss. Gorky was treated in Capri.

⌒

Chekhov died at forty-four. Since the age of twenty-eight, he had suffered from insomnia, and he treated it by drinking a bottle of beer every night, often of bad quality. He thought that he was descended from the artisan Andrei Chokhov, who cast the colossal cannon (the czar of cannons, which never succeeded in firing) that is in the garden of the Kremlin, near the czar of bells, an enormous bell, broken during casting, which never succeeded in ringing—symbols, in Chekhov's words, of that "Russian tendency to spend money in the construction of every sort of uselessness when the most pressing human needs are not yet satisfied."

"The best Russian writer is Chekhov," W. H. Auden said, "because he is the only one who has the least bit of common sense." Except for the common sense, Auden is right. Tolstoy read aloud to his family a story of Chekhov's, and fell asleep on the manuscript of *Fathers and Sons,* which Turgenev had given him to read.

In 1894 Chekhov was in Milan. He saw the Duomo and the Galleria Vittorio Emanuele, and visited the crematorium—"that is, the cemetery where they burn the dead." He wanted to go to Como, but he had to give it up because it was too hot on the lake. His grandfather had been a serf.

Chekhov also concerned himself with toilets. It is well known, he says, that the Russians hold this type of comfort in disdain. "In the villages there are no toilets at all; in monasteries, at fairs, in inns, and in every type of industry . . . they are absolutely disgusting." In Siberia the toilet was nothing more than a big stick: for defense against wolves.

In the course of a journey Chekhov slept, for lack of anything better, in a second-class railway carriage abandoned on a disused track. "During the night," he writes, "I got down from the carriage for a little need, and outside was an authentic marvel. . . . The moon, the limitless steppe with the tumuli, and the desert; a silence of the tomb; the wagons and the wheels that stood out shining in the shadow. The world seemed dead."

In Russia, the chamber pot was called Yakov

Andreyich—that is, James, the son of Andrew. Andrew must therefore be considered the father of the chamber pot. It had a human name, as it does also with us Italians: Giüli (Julius) in Lombardy and Zi'Peppe (Uncle Joe) in Lazio. The chamber pot was a luxury. Toilets, when there were any, were almost always in the courtyard, and to get up at night and go out into the cold was a dangerous undertaking. "At night it is a true martyrdom," Chekhov says. "Darkness, wind, doors that squeak and are hard to open, wanderings through the dim courtyard, a suspicious silence, no newspaper."

Fortunately, the good Yakov Andreyich sometimes peeked out from beneath the bed. It even happened that a young servant boy would sit for a few minutes on the pot to warm the edge for his master. "Yakov Andreyich," Chekhov says, "resembled a tureen and was decorated with friezes in delicate mezzotints."

⤳

Widespread among the muzhiks was the custom, probably from China, of beating their wives, even for no reason. In a popular song the mother says, "What a son, what a head of the family you are! You don't beat your wife, who is young. . . ."

Soldiers, government employees, students all wore uniforms. Nicholas II prescribed even the color of the material for the dresses of the maids of honor and lady companions of the empress.

The Russians called trousers "United States of America."

Before leaving on a journey they would close themselves in a room and sit for some minutes in silence, without looking at each other.

Servants kissed their masters on the shoulder. At Christmas they would dress as bears, Turks, innkeepers, and ladies, and dance in the drawing room.

Other widespread maladies: hemorrhoids, which a friend of Chekhov's cured by keeping a chestnut from an Indian chestnut tree in a pocket of his trousers, and petechial typhus, caused by the immense number of lice then living in Russia, which equaled the number of bedbugs and cockroaches. The louse was General Kutuzov's most powerful ally against Napoleon and, after the victory, deserved, like him, to receive from the czar the order of St. George of the first class and a monument on the Nevsky Prospect.

Vodka was a remedy for many evils. The proverb says: "Against troubles, vodka inside and vodka outside." Against infections, vodka with hot pepper; against toothache, vodka with horseradish. "The first little glass of vodka suffocates you," says the Russian drinker; "the second makes you bold, like a falcon; after the third the glasses fly like birds."

The best-quality vodka came in bottles whose corks were sealed with white wax, vodka of poorer quality in bottles sealed with red wax. When the landowner gave vodka to his peasants, or the officer to his soldiers, it was measured in buckets. The bucket was a precise measure: 12.29 liters. In restaurants the unit of measure was the gram. You ordered fifty or a hundred grams.

Alcoholism was widespread among rich and poor. The vice of drinking was called a "weakness." The speeches of the inebriated were a resource for writers—Pushkin and Dostoyevsky in particular (the marvelous rambling on of the drunk Korovkin which ends "The Village of Stepanchikovo"). There are many kinds of vodka:

Limonnaya, with lemon,

Kubanskaya, from Kuban,

Moskovskaya, from Moscow,

Kazanskaya, from Kazan—"where the trams were drawn by camels" (Shklovsky)—with a Cossack on horseback on the label.

Pertsovka, with hot pepper. This vodka was the principal purpose of coming to Moscow for a Roman citizen, who always carried with him on the journey, in an inside jacket pocket, a package of powdered Calabrian hot pepper, which he sprinkled liberally on whatever food, dry or in broth, was set before him, even before he knew what it was, and which he then offered courteously to his fellow diners, much as, in the railway stations of Chekhov's time, travelers offered a powder for keeping off bedbugs to ladies who faced a night on the benches of the waiting room, behind a screen.

Koriandrovaya, with coriander,

Zubrovka, with bison grass,

Okhotnichya, of the hunter,

Stolichnaya, of the capital,

vodka with anise,

vodka with saffron,

Georgian vodka.

"Good vodka! How is it made?"

"With an infusion of cockroaches!" (Chekhov).

Gorilka, the Ukrainian vodka, which is drunk in a glass bearing the inscription "Even the monks drink it."

Starka, seasoned,

Krepkaya, strong,

gooseberry vodka, which is accompanied by *va-trushki,* sweet fritters served with hot antipasti,

vodka with horseradish,

vodka with juniper,

vodka with sorb apples, Esenin's favorite; and sweet vodka (for ladies), bitter vodka, pink vodka, dark vodka . . .

There are so many kinds of vodka because there are so many tastes. As the proverb says, "Some like the Pope and some the Pòpadia [the Pope's wife]." Gogol describes the color of dark vodka thus: "An olivelike color, the color that is found only in those transparent Siberian stones in which, in Russia, seals are carved."

One can pour vodka from a single bottle or make a mixture of two or three different kinds.

One can drink without eating anything. In this case the model is offered by the degenerate Count Karneyev, of Chekhov's "The Shooting Party": "The waiter Ilya brought on a silver tray a tiny glass of vodka and half a glass of plain water. The Count drank the vodka in one gulp, then the water."

Or else eat, immediately after drinking, an appropriate morsel: like the doctor Andrei Yefimich Ragin—

spied on, one might say, by Chekhov while he was immersed in reading. "Beside his book there is always a small decanter of vodka and a salted cucumber. . . . Every half hour, without raising his eyes from the book, he fills a little glass with vodka and drinks; then, without looking, gropes for the cucumber and bites off a piece of it."

But the best thing to eat after a glass of vodka is a piece of smoked sturgeon (*balyk*)—the only Russian dish to be praised by Gide during his visit to the U.S.S.R. in 1936. Céline, who arrived there the same year, found nothing good at all: "I don't like their cooking . . . I don't like their sunflower oil . . . it is the alimentary system of a neglected prison . . . the salted cucumbers are indigestible . . . the cockroaches . . ."

Dumas *père*—who understood more about cooking than Gide and Céline—in his *Grand Dictionnaire de Cuisine* speaks with nostalgia of a sturgeon soup called *ouka,* a very expensive food for the rich. He says he wrote to Russia for the recipe, but as far as is known he never received it. The best sturgeon are the small ones (which used to be cooked in silver pans), but they can reach enormous dimensions—like one caught in 1769 that was sixty feet long and weighed two thousand three hundred and ten pounds. It was worthy of being exhibited in the elegant windows of Milyutin, on the Nevsky Prospect—which at that time were well stocked—perhaps along with "cherries for five rubles each," or "a gigantic watermelon, as big as a carriage," as Gogol says, and other costly gastronomic rarities, destined, unfortunately, only to be looked at with longing by the great majority of the passersby. Today in the windows there are no cherries for five rubles each— only, as Céline said, "an immense heap of useless junk . . . absolutely unsellable except in Russia."

⟿

The word one encounters most often in the classics of Russian literature is "cabbage," followed by "cucumber." "Cabbage-eater" is what the Russian is called in America, as the Frenchman is called "frog," short for "frog-eater," frogs being something that Anglo-Saxons refuse to eat. Escoffier succeeded in making his aristocratic clients at the Savoy in London eat frogs' legs only by hiding them on the menu under the name *Nymphes à l'aurore*; it was a cold dish, in aspic, that had a great success.

For Russians, cabbage is the principal food. It is

served at almost every meal, as a first course, second course, vegetable, salad, perhaps dessert: cabbage soup (*shchi*), borscht, cabbage-filled rolls (*pirozhki*), cabbage pie à la Muscovite (*pirog*), sauerkraut with mushrooms, red cabbage, sauerkraut tart, etc. The smell of cabbage soup impregnates public offices. Cabbage in Russia is eternal. The muzhik says, "The worm eats the cabbage and dies before the cabbage."

In a few words Chekhov sketches the portrait of a Russian eater: "On his beard he had little pieces of cabbage, and he gave off the odor of vodka." "What I desire," said Pushkin, "is quiet and a pot of cabbage soup, the biggest possible."

Shchi (*shchi lenivye*) is the cabbage soup of Great Russia, capital Moscow, and of White Russia (Byelorussia), capital Minsk. The adjective *lenivy* means "lazy," "idle," "sluggish," or, as Gogol would say, "smoker of the sky," perhaps intending to show how little work the preparation of this soup requires, especially when the poor make it: water, salt, and cabbage.

Other dishes of the kitchens of the poor: black bread soaked in water, bread and salt with kvass, bread and onions. "What shall we eat? A first-rate meal. First course, bread and kvass; second course, kvass and bread" (Tolstoy). For the convicts who worked in the mines of Sakhalin: turnips or tallow candles. The muzhiks said, "We look at the same sun, but we don't eat the same thing."

Borscht, on the other hand, is the cabbage soup of Little Russia (Ukraine), capital Kiev, a country of heavy eaters, where a chicken is considered a simple appetizer, where the best sausages are made, and where the proverb "The best bird is the sausage" was born.

In Great Russia at one time it was said that while the borscht was cooking, the Ukrainians threw into the pot some azure five-ruble notes or pink ten-ruble ones, preferably worn by use, to make the soup more tasty. The characteristic of borscht is to be colored red by the juice of its beets and veined white by the sour cream added at the last minute. Above all, says Zilin, the secretary of the College of Justices of the Peace, and at mealtimes an irresistible evoker of the delights of Russian cooking, "cabbage soup must be very hot, scalding" (Chekhov).

☙

In the penitentiary of Omsk, in Siberia, where Dostoyevsky spent four years, the thin cabbage soup (water and cabbage), besides not being very hot, was served with cockroaches. Cockroaches, along with bed-

bugs, were then so common in houses that their presence on a plate did not prevent the soup from being
eaten. "Our peasant," says Chekhov, "blows with re-
pugnance on the kvass in which there are cockroaches,
and nonetheless drinks it." (Kvass is a fermented drink
made from rye and malt; Napoleon's troops called it
limonade de cochon but did not despise it.)

When they are so many, cockroaches and bedbugs
are no longer silent but produce what Chekhov calls "a
murmuring and a noisy rustling": "The walls and ceiling [of the *isba*] were covered by a black crepe that
moved as if stirred by the wind; from some parts of the
crepe that moved rapidly forward and back one could
guess of what this living, mobile mass consisted; one
heard a murmuring and a noisy rustling as if the cockroaches and bedbugs were in a great hurry and were
conversing with one another."

In comparison, this from *War and Peace* is a summer
idyll: "A cricket cried across the passage, on the street
someone was shouting and singing, the cockroaches rus-
tled on the table, on the icons, and on the walls."

Perhaps in order to feel closer to his muzhiks, at a
costume ball Tolstoy disguised himself as a cockroach.

☞

In Chekhov's letters to his beloved wife Olga "cockroach" becomes a tender word of love:

"My treasure, little cockroach . . ."

"I embrace my little cockroach and kiss it a million times. . . ."

Nor does he stop at "little cockroach":

"I kiss my little bug."

"I embrace my little turkey."

"My little mosquito."

"My dear pony . . ."

"My little sperm whale, treasure . . ."

But the animal that Chekhov referred to most often on these occasions was the dog.

"My dear little dog."

"My little bitch."

"I embrace my dear, my lovely dachshund."

Less comprehensible is the word "dog" pure and simple.

"My soul, angel, my dog, little dove . . ."

"My little treasure, dog, my Olyusha . . ."

Olga survived the author of the letters by many years. She died at Yalta, on the Black Sea, "city of Tartars and hairdressers," scene of the story "The Lady with the Little Dog." With Chekhov's sister, she lived in the house where Chekhov had resided for some years: the modest house of a great writer where there are no books—a thing less strange than it appears at first sight. In the medicine chest Chekhov kept a revolver.

In the Crimea Chekhov saw an ideal house: "A house with four rooms, a little house of Tartar design, a kitchen, a stable for the cows, a drying room for tobacco, a spring rising from the rocks, a cart, a scale, a cupboard, a wardrobe, two tables, a dozen Viennese chairs, a sofa, an iron stove." No bed. "My dream," he wrote in another letter, "is to build—in the woods that I already own—a house, to plant roses, to give orders that I will receive no one, and to write short stories."

Few memories are left of the Yalta of Chekhov's time: the villas, the mansions of those days are crumbling, the gardens have grown wild. The cockroaches remain.

One of Chekhov's best stories is about a dog with a reddish coat called Kashtanka (Chestnut), which was the name of a dog he had in his house. The cat of the house was called Fyodor Timofeyich: a name and a patronymic, as if he were an Orthodox Christian—that is, Theodore, the son of a former cat, Timothy.

The most common name for dogs is Sharik, a

diminutive of the word "ball" (that is, Little Ball), just as for cats the most common name is Vaska, and for bears it is Misha (Mike). Sharik is the good black-and-white dog in the prison where Dostoyevsky was shut up, which no one looked at or caressed except him; in *The House of the Dead* he wrote, "A Russian, usually, does not believe in feeding dogs."

Esenin says:

> O sister bitches, brother dogs,
> Men persecute me like you.

⇝

Like cabbages, cucumbers are an essential vegetable for Russians. Céline says, "Over there, man fills his belly with cucumbers," and Saltykov Shchedrin, the satirist, sententiously, "Man needs everything: butter, cabbages, cucumbers."

Inasmuch as cucumbers are made almost entirely of water, they have in Russia virtues unknown to us: "He gave me some water and a cucumber"—that is, more water—"to refresh myself" (Leskov). "In the event of inhaling charcoal fumes cover the head with pickled cucumbers and tie a cloth around it" (Goncharov).

Also surprising is the use that Russian writers make of the cucumber as a term of comparison: the Prince (*Anna Karenina*) "had always a freshness that could be compared to that of a big Dutch cucumber, green and bright." Even a beautiful girl can be compared (by Chekhov) to a cucumber: "You are very pretty. . . . You remind me of a fresh salted cucumber; that, so to speak, still tastes of the hothouse but already is a little salty and has the perfume of dill."

The cucumber in Russian is *ogurets,* the cabbage *kapusta.* Other names in Russian cooking: *zakuski, pirozhki, solyanka, okroshka.* . . . *Zakuski* are appetizers, the glory of Russian cuisine, which, according to Ivan P. Guryanov, the former director of Moscow's Sovetsky Restaurant, included ten thousand dishes. Professor Filip Filipovich Preobrazhenski remembered nostalgically the hot appetizers of the Slavyansky Bazaar, a restaurant (and hotel) in Moscow which one meets often in the pages of Russian literature; a character in Chekhov's masterpiece "Peasants" worked there as a waiter for many years, before retiring to end his days in the misery of his native village. Famous names: blini Demidov, cream Malakov, saddle of veal Orlov, beef Stroganoff. A letter from a friend in New York: "Some days ago at the house of friends I had the Russian dish *coulibiac,* a pie of meats, cabbage and mushrooms, herbs, spices—a delight. The pastry on top and underneath was perfect. I had more than one piece. It was picnic fare."

⇐

The first Russian restaurant has opened in Milan. The Russian tongue doesn't seem so abstruse anymore: *restoran, menu, vino, sardini, omlet, antrekot, eskalop, file, kotlet, bifstek, rosbif, fazan, kartofel, ris, pomidory, tort, kompot, ananas, banan, limon, mandarin.* . . . Bread and salt, brothers! (*Bon appétit!*)

In Milan we also have the Kremlin, the Kremlin of our great writer Carlo Emilio Gadda: "Near the new polytechnic . . . rises a building somewhat theatrical, sharp and rocklike, but above all foolish, popularly called the Kremlin." It is called the Kremlin probably because of its two spires, which recall, rather, Petersburg, or, even more, those pretentious cement spires raised on simple dwellings in Leningrad, under the reign of Joseph the Terrible, in imitation of the gilded "Dutch" spires of Petersburg.

When the doorkeeper's clock of our Kremlin says ten, the carillon of the great black-and-gold English clock on the Spasskaya tower in Moscow sounds midday. The tourists stand motionless, "like horses being put in harness" (Goncharov), and an enormous flock of croaking crows rises in flight from the walls, fluttering over Red Square.

III

In 1703 Peter the Great founded the new capital, naming it, in the German style, Sanktpeterburg (Saintpetersburg), City of St. Peter. The name was then divided in two, becoming St. Petersburg, and giving the impression that there exists a saint by the name of Petersburg. Along the way the saint was lost, and Petersburg remained: the city of Czar Peter, Slavonicized in 1914 to Petrograd. But the name, too long for the Petersburgers, had already been shortened to Peter.

Peter the Great was the son of Alexis the Mild, who had seven thousand rebels exterminated at one time and the head of Stenka Razin cut off. Peter himself, during the last revolt of his praetorians, had seven hundred and ninety-nine of them hanged in Moscow. Nabokov, without letting himself be influenced by the enthusiasm of Voltaire, called him an "arch-bully."

When, at the suggestion of his court jester Yakov (an ancestor of Turgenev), Peter with his own hand cut off the beards—a symbol of backwardness—of the boyars, it was not a jest. Taking the scissors in hand, he knew he was risking life and throne. There was a distant echo of this undertaking in America when Lionel Barrymore said of Louis B. Mayer, of M-G-M: "He would cut off the beard of Tolstoy."

Peter had thin black whiskers. He was almost six and a half feet tall. His gigantic boots, which fascinated Lenin, are preserved in the Kremlin; at the Hermitage is his worktable, which is very high, because he used to write standing up. The "Bible of Peter the Great" is a leather box in the form of a big volume, which contains six bottles. He dressed carelessly. "He had patches on his bottom," says (approximately) Marina Svetayeva. "He liked German beer and strong Knaster tobacco." He was very strong and could bend a silver coin with his fingers. He died young, at fifty-one. "When his bier was opened, after the revolution, he was still there, entire and undamaged" (Joseph Roth). Ready, one might say, to be transferred to the mausoleum in Red Square.

The same thing happened to the father of the Italian writer Antonio Delfini, who died even younger than

Peter the Great—at thirty. Delfini was present at the opening of the bier. "I believe I am the only person in the world," he wrote later, "to whom such a thing has happened: the only son of fifty who has seen his father of thirty."

Peter the Great created the *chin*—the table of hierarchies, of ranks. All the employees of the State were divided into fourteen categories:

1. Chancellor of the State
2. Regular Privy Counselor
3. Privy Counselor
4. Regular Counselor of State
5. Counselor of State
6. Collegiate Counselor
7. Court Counselor
8. Collegiate Assessor
9. Titular Counselor
10. Collegiate Secretary
11. Naval Secretary
12. Government Secretary
13. Registrar of the Senate, of the Synod, and of the Cabinet
14. Collegiate Registrar.

Every rank had its title. The privy counselor was "Excellency"; the sixth, seventh, and eighth ranks were "High Nobility," etc. Every rank had its special uniform, on which the greatest possible number of decorations, of the first, second, and third class, were displayed, on the chest, hanging around the neck, or even on the scabbard of the saber: the order of St. Andrew, instituted by Peter the Great; the order of St. Vladimir, the order of St. George, the order of St. Stanislaus and that of St. Anna, established by the Duke of Holstein-Gottorp in memory of the Empress Anna, which Tolstoy received after he fought in the Crimean War (which signaled the end of his military career), and many others. The father of Dostoyevsky, a modest doctor at the Hospital for the Poor in Moscow, had collected a cross of St. Vladimir of the fourth class, a cross of St. Anna of the third class, and a cross of St. Anna of the second class.

After the première of *La Forza del Destino* at the Imperial Theater in Petersburg, Verdi was made Commander of the Imperial and Royal Order of St. Stanislaus. He put the badge in his suitcase, but in Russia decorations are worn every day, even on trains, even at work. Turgenev's Panshin walked "with a slight stoop, perhaps because of the decoration of St. Vladimir 'on his neck,' which weighed him down, drawing him toward the ground"; and little Helen, of *The Insulted and Injured*, while the doctor was visiting her, "could only gaze fixedly at the enormous order of St. Stanislaus hanging around his neck."

Platon Kuzmich Kovalyov ("The Nose") was a collegiate assessor, but as a title of the Caucasus this was, of course, of minor value, like degrees from certain universities; therefore he introduced himself as Major Kovalyov. His nose, on the other hand, which had mysteriously abandoned his face and transformed itself into an independent human being, seemed from its dress to be a counselor of state: embroidered gold uniform with a tall standup collar, chamois pants, sword, and plumed hat.

⌒

In Petersburg (in summer, "sultriness, dust, strange smells . . .") three streets converge—forming the so-called Trident—on the tall gold spire of the Admiralty, which Chekhov compares, for leanness and thinness, to the titular counselor Kraterov.

On the left is the Prospect of the Ascension

(Voznesensky Prospect)—the Prospect V. of *Crime and Punishment,* where, in a deserted courtyard, Raskolnikov hid the profits of his crime, and where, Gogol says, lived the barber Ivan Yakovlevich, on whose shop sign was painted "a man with his cheeks soaped and the legend 'Also lets blood.' "

Signs, illustrated so that they would be understood by the illiterate, formed, along the sidewalks of the city, a permanent show of the kind of popular painting dear to Magritte—a show that, unfortunately, thanks to compulsory education, has disappeared. Gogol particularly liked barbers' signs. "Grigory Grigorevich," he writes in *Evenings on a Farm near Dikanka,* "sat down in his usual place at the head of the table, covering himself with an enormous napkin and becoming like those heroes whom barbers have painted on their signs."

Grigory Grigorevich reminds me of an uncle from Sondrio, a country town at the foot of the Alps, a man as good as gold, whom a misfortune had made a little absentminded. Like Grigory Grigorevich, he used to sit at the head of the table, but he would get there far too early, when it was still quite a while until dinnertime. The stoves had not yet been lighted, and the uncle, sitting in his place and covered by the napkin, was already waiting. After a bit, he would begin to look around, to drum with his fingers on the tablecloth. "But here," as Gogol would say, "a thick fog shrouds the story."

In the center of the Trident is Gorokhovaya Ulitsa, the Street of Peas, where, in a house "whose population would have been sufficient for a whole country town," lived Ilya Ilyich Oblomov, the illustrious symbol of Russian laziness. With him lived the old servant Zakhar, roosting permanently on the stove, to which he retired like a bear to his den, and the other usual inhabitants of those mansions: bugs, cockroaches, and mice.

Goncharov—the author of *Oblomov*—and Lenin were both born in the distant city of Simbirsk, on the Volga, which, in honor of Lenin, is now called Ulyanovsk. Said Oblomov, "I have never put on stockings by myself, as long as I have lived, thank God," and Lenin said, "The aim of my life is to fight Oblomovism." Behind Oblomovism he saw millions of Russians used to doing nothing, "incapable," as Trotsky says, "of doing anything without the lower classes, without the work force, without men for cannon fodder, without orderlies, maids, quartermasters, drivers, porters, cooks, washerwomen, signalmen, telegraphists, grooms, coachmen."

One of the last streets that crosses the Street of Peas is the wide Morskaya Ulitsa, the home of elegant hairdressers' shops. No. 47 is a mansion of rosy granite, ennobled by a coat of arms representing, one might say, the soul of Russia—two bears holding up a chessboard—and there, with his family, served by fifty servants, lived little Vladimir Vladimirovich Nabokov, destined to write and to die in exile. Vronsky lived on the same street. The Revolution replaced peas with the Polish Feliks Dzerzhinsky, the first Soviet Minister of the Interior and the head of the Cheka, whom Nabokov associates with his more sadly known successor, General Yagoda. From home, Vladimir Vladimirovich was taken by automobile to the aristocratic Tenishev school—where, a few years before, Mandelstam had studied—in Mokhovaya Ulitsa, the Street of Mosses, which recalls (or would recall, if, as I think, even this lovely name has disappeared) the marshes on which the city was built: so do Kozoye Boloto (Goat Marshes), Peski (the Sands), where Dostoyevsky lived, the Bolotnaya (Swamp Street), etc. According to Shklovsky, a begging dog used to occupy the corner of Mokhovaya Ulitsa and Simyonskaya Ulitsa.

Chekhov recounts how "a noted poet, proceeding along the Mokhovaya, where the University was, lowered the window of the carriage and spit at the University." The reason for his contempt, expressed in a typically Russian manner, is not reported. "The coachman," Chekhov says, "was so accustomed to this that whenever he passed the University he stopped."

In Moscow, too, there was a Mokhovaya Ulitsa: it is where the starving and mangy bastard of "Heart of a Dog," Sharik, learns to decipher the letters of the Cyrillic alphabet, using as a textbook the sign over a fish market. Thus Mayakovsky:

> I learned the alphabet from signs,
> turning pages of iron and tin.

Finally, on the right of the Trident is the most famous street in Russia, the Prospect of the Neva, the Nevsky Prospect. The ignorant, servants and coachmen, said "Prespekt."

The Trident has its model in Rome. The three streets—Via di Ripetta, Via del Corso, and Via del Babuino—converge on the obelisk of Piazza del Popolo rather than on the slender spire of the Admiralty. Gogol, descending the Spanish Steps from Via Sistina, where he was living, and where he was writing the "poem" of *Dead Souls,* continued his walk by setting off along the Nevsky Prospect (Via del Babuino), at the foot of which was a glimpse, on the right, of the Hôtel de Russie. A herd of goats was resting in the middle of the street.

❧

In 1912, eighteen thousand carriages and sleds were ready to parade along the Nevsky Prospect. In winter, with the snow, the silvery jingle of horses' bells was the only sound animating the streets of the capital, and the coachmen, "with their enormous behinds" (and their horses), were, even if they did not know it, important personages. A worker of the time, speaking of what characterizes a city, says, "There must be great mansions . . . a theater, the police . . . coachmen. . . ."

"All coachmen," Dostoyevsky says, "have a taciturn and imperturbable character, as if, indeed, the continuous contact with horses roused in man a particular seriousness, or rather, you might say, gravity." But they were ready to brutally whip passersby who did not get out of their way, as happened to Raskolnikov on the bridge over the Neva, and as, many years before, had happened in London to Gulliver, when he returned from Lilliput. Coachmen carried a clock, mounted in leather and secured to the back of their belt, to provide the exact time for passengers, and a thin cord was attached to their elbow, which the passenger could pull to make the carriage stop, as if it were a tram. To rein in the horses they emitted a special sound: "*Tprr.*" They accompanied their masters (and clients) to parties, dinners, theaters, and waited for them outside in the cold, for hours. Only in the most frequented places were there shelters heated by bonfires.

Verdi's wife, who in 1862 was with the maestro in Petersburg for the première of *Forza,* wrote in a letter, "The poor in general and the coachmen in particular are the unhappiest creatures in the universe."

A coachman different (in part) from the others was Timofey, the son of Tolstoy by one of his peasants, whom Tolstoy never acknowledged, although Timofey was, of all his sons, the one who most resembled him. Timofey served at Yasnaya Polyana as coachman. He mounted the box and asked his father, "Where do you wish me to take you, *barin* [master]?"

For his sojourn in the Russian capital Verdi brought along a hundred small bottles of Bordeaux table wine (a wine that Captain Potseluyev, of *Dead Souls,* called simply *burdashka*); twenty bottles of good Bordeaux; and twenty bottles of champagne. He was also a hearty eater. Here is the menu of the meal served to him in Milan on January 7, 1901, a few weeks before his death, by the devoted waiter Umberto Bertolazzi: "Risotto alla certosina, boiled sea bass with mayonnaise, braised beef, lamb cutlets, meat 'alla parmigiana,' roast turkey, salad, dessert, fruit, rum ice cream." Verdi ate everything—in small amounts, of course, but he did taste every dish. Risotto "alla certosina" (with shrimp, and perhaps frogs and mushrooms) was his favorite risotto, which sometimes he would cook himself, very well, it seems, when he was at home, in Sant'Agata—I was about to say Yasnaya Polyana.

At No. 17 of the Prospect rises the mansion of the rich Count Stroganov, from whose kitchens, in all probability, came the recipe for beef Stroganoff. The present version of this dish—using not filet but very tough meat, cut by an ax striking the sort of blows the executioner who decapitated Stenka Razin on the round stone in Red Square would have been able to make—is, sadly, far from the original, and would make the poor Count turn in his grave. By chance, however, the dish ended up among the thousand recipes of the popular cookbook of Frate Indovino, under the Vernean name of beef Strogoff. Ingredients: beef, potatoes, onions, butter, salt, pepper, and yogurt, replacing the sour cream (*smetana*), which is still little known in Italian cooking. "It is a recipe of Tatiana Pavlova," says the author, "and constitutes a dish very tasty and very . . . Russian." The three dots summarize his diffidence concerning this cuisine. From Russian cooking, he seems to say, we must expect anything.

The Stroganov mansion is at the corner of the Prospect and the Moika canal, where Prince Yusupov threw Rasputin, who had survived poison and pistol shots. Throwing people into the Moika was a custom. Dolokhov, Pierre, and their companions (*War and Peace*) seized the commissar of police, who was hurrying to arrest them, bound him shoulder to shoulder with a bear, and threw the pair into the Moika. Thieves were thrown into the Fontanka.

In Gogol's time, on the Prospect, at the hour of the greatest crowds—between two and three in the afternoon, before lunch—one could see the nose of Collegiate Assessor Kovalyov passing in its carriage, and on foot Kovalyov himself, hiding with a handkerchief his shameful lack of a nose, and (who knows?) Titular

Counselor Akaky Akakyevich with his new overcoat. They strolled among the crowd—on the sonorous wooden sidewalks—"among raccoon coats and beaver collars" (Goncharov), skirting the Europe Hotel, the luxurious food emporium of the brothers Eliseyev, the sparkling windows of Milyutin, the famous French restaurants and Swiss cafés, where Pushkin, as everyone knows, drank his last lemonade, and Tolstoy, leaving for the Crimea, left debts. They mixed with Great and Little Russians, White Russians, Tartars, crows, elegant French masters of language and of cooking, Germans with unmarked waistlines, land administrators, tutors, craftsmen, doctors, Finnish wet nurses, Italian architects and dancing masters. Gogol says, "There is nothing more beautiful than the Prospect, at least in Petersburg." Dostoyevsky will think of it differently: "The broad, tedious street of Petersburg, exactly like a taut string." For Trotsky it will be merely "the main artery of the bourgeoisie."

Anyway, the Prospect soon began to decline. "From 1836," Gogol also says, "this noisy street, in constant agitation, bustling and chattering, was completely out of favor; now the promenade is along the Neva, on the Riverside of the English."

On the wooden sidewalk (which today no longer exists) of the Prospect, where on Sundays the drunken peasants lay sleeping, Zoshchenko saw Esenin coming toward him. Elegant, pallid, with lifeless eyes. They entered a beer hall. "Esenin says something to the waiter. And he brings him a glass of sorb-apple vodka. Esenin closes his eyes, drinks. And," says Zoshchenko, "I see how with every swallow life returns to him. His cheeks become rosier, his gestures more assured, his eyes shine."

> Better in fact
> > to die of vodka
> Than of boredom!

Mayakovsky had said to him. But neither of them died of vodka. Esenin slit his wrists, in 1925, in a hotel room. He was thirty years old. Mayakovsky killed himself hastily five years later. At thirty-six he was stung by "the wasp of a bullet" in his office in Moscow, near the great Dzerzhinsky Square, with its gloomy monument to Dzerzhinsky—of which only the base remains— where the Mayakovsky Museum is now.

In Dzerzhinsky Square begins Kirov Street, where, at No. 39, is the former Tsentrosoyuz, the only building in Russia designed by Le Corbusier. Corbu (that is, crow)—a nickname that in the land of crows should have brought him luck—also entered the contest for the Palace of the Soviets, but without success. His architecture was exactly the opposite of Stalinist architecture, which, with the passage of time, begins to exert a strange, perverse Asian fascination.

Vladimir Vladimirovich, "latrine cleaner and water carrier drafted by the Revolution," was a Georgian, like Stalin, with penetrating eyes, like those of Picasso. He was born in Bagdady, a beautiful Oriental name that recalls Baghdad. That name was deleted and replaced by Mayakovsky. According to Marina Svetayeva, Mayakovsky was two things at the same time: "He is the driver and also the horse."

⤻

At the end of the Nevsky Prospect is Alexander Nevsky Square (Alexander Yaroslavovich, the liberator of Russia, was called Nevsky after his victory over the Swedes, in 1240, on the banks of the Neva), with the great convent and the church dedicated to him (he was canonized by the Orthodox Church), and two ancient cemeteries, in one of which, Tikhvin, rests Dostoyevsky, who had begged his wife not to bury him in the Volkovskoye cemetery among the literati. ("I do not want to lie in the middle of my enemies.") Around Dostoyevsky are Glinka, Mussorgsky, Rimsky-Korsakov, Borodin, Tchaikovsky. Dostoyevsky had never shown a particular inclination toward music; he appreciated Beethoven, Mendelssohn, and Rossini and could not bear Wagner. Destiny wished him to have as neighbors in death, besides his friend Nekrasov, the greatest musicians of Russia. After our companions in school, in military service, in hospital or prison, these are our final companions.

In the other cemetery the Neapolitan architect Carlo (Ivanovich) Rossi is buried. Besides the false, unreliable arch (the Arch of the General Headquarters), on which gallops the six-horse carriage of Victory, as Solzhenitsyn says, Rossi built Teatralnaya Ulitsa (which now bears his name), in which he tried to realize a street with perfect proportions—the dream of an alchemist rather than an architect. It is twenty-two meters wide, and is flanked by buildings each of which is twenty-two meters high and two hundred and twenty meters long. It would have pleased Gadda, who objected to the irregularities of the Milanese streets and admired the ugly but regular Via Dante.

All traces of the tomb of Giacomo Quarenghi, Catherine the Great's architect, who was born near Bergamo and died in Petersburg in 1817, vanished. It was rediscovered only in 1966, and now Quarenghi rests not far from Carlo Rossi. It is a well-deserved repose, if one thinks of everything the illustrious Bergamask architect built in thirty-eight years of work. Dzhakomo Kvarengi "worked like a horse," wrote Catherine, using a typical Russian comparison of the time. He worked like those Bergamasks one meets at night on the Milan–Bergamo railway line. They get up before dawn to go to their jobs in Milan, and return at night to Bergamo; a bus takes them home, where, as soon as they finish dinner, "murderous slumber lays upon them his leaden mace." So says Shakespeare—to whom Tolstoy preferred Harriet Beecher Stowe, the author of *Uncle Foma's Isba*.

"The good Quarenghi," as the poet Pindemonte calls him, had a large, typically Bergamask face, pouting and cordial at the same time, with a giant potato nose in the middle, probably reddened by vodka, a target for caricaturists. Meeting him on the Nevsky, Collegiate Assessor Kovalyov would have taken him for his own nose.

When spring arrived at Yasnaya Polyana and Tolstoy said, "I am going to the Nevsky Prospect," he meant that he was going to a road at the edge of his property to watch the groups of muzhiks passing, going off on pilgrimages; and surely he wished to join them. ("Their beards have a wonderful aroma of spring.")

☞

Gorky (Aleksei Maksimovich Peshkov) was much—too much—esteemed by Lenin, who could not bear Dostoyevsky, and by Stalin. Gide, too, exaggerated, in the speech he gave in Red Square at the funeral of the writer: "No Russian writer has been more universally heard. . . . He takes his place beside the greatest."

Tolstoy was a better judge: "*The Mother* is worthless." Also, Chekhov: "I read the end of *The Three,* Gorky's novel. It's really outlandish. If it hadn't been written by Gorky, no one would read it." He was a friend of Gorky's but saw his defects clearly. "Another piece of advice," he wrote him in a letter. "Reading the proofs, delete, wherever possible, the adjectives and adverbs. You use so many adjectives that the reader has a hard time finding his way, and gets tired."

Gorky means "bitter."

"It's bitter!" is the cry (and an order) that resounds continuously during wedding feasts.

"But excuse me, what on earth is this? The herring is bitter . . . and the bread is bitter. One cannot eat!"

All: "It's bitter, it's bitter!" The newlyweds kiss. (Chekhov, *The Wedding*.)

The life of Gorky from the age of ten to twenty-four in a very brief autobiographical note: "1878: cobbler's assistant. 1879: apprentice draftsman. 1880: dishwasher on a ship. 1884: errand boy. 1885: baker. 1886: chorus boy in an operetta company. 1887: I try to kill myself. 1890: copyist for a lawyer. 1891: I make a tour of Russia on foot. 1892: I publish my first novel."

It is not the only tumultuous biography of that tumultuous epoch.

Isaac Babel, 1894–1941.

"I have been a soldier on the Romanian front, an employee in the Cheka and in the Commissariat of Public Instruction, I took part in the food requisitions of 1918, served in the Northern Army against General Yudenich, in the First Cavalry Army, and in the Odessa regional Soviet, then I worked as a newspaper reporter in Petersburg and Tiflis and as a copy editor in the 7th Soviet Printing Plant in Odessa, and so on." (Marc Slonim, *Soviet Russian Literature*.)

In 1941 he was shot.

Mikhail Zoshchenko, 1895–1958.

"I was a carpenter, a hunter on the island of Nova Zemlya, an apprentice cobbler, a telephone operator, a policeman at the Ligovo station, an agent on the criminal squad, an actor, and again I went as a volunteer to the front with the Red Army.

"Here is an arid list of the events that concern me:

death sentences: one,

wounds: three,

suicides: two,

beatings: three." (Preface to the Italian translation of *Before the Sunrise.*)

Two suicides seems excessive, even for those difficult times. The same notes, which also precede the Italian edition of the beautiful *Muscovite Tales* (a strange title for stories that do not take place in Moscow), mention instead "two homicide attempts." Most likely, it is a matter of suicide attempts, as in the case of Gorky.

When it was decided to give back to Gorky Ulitsa (the main street of Moscow) its old name of Tverskaya—that is, the way to Tver—a problem arose: Tverskaya led no longer to Tver but to Kalinin, as Tver had been rebaptized. So Kalinin also got its old name back, and thus the problem was solved.

Dostoyevsky was confined at Tver after his years in Siberia and before receiving permission to return to Petersburg, and there he wrote *The Village of Stepanchikovo and Its Inhabitants*: after the horrors of the penitentiary, a humorous novel.

The novel's protagonist, Foma Fomich, is a character who could have existed only in the Russia of landed proprietors and serfs: the parasite—"whom Russian literature," Tolstoy says, "holds, no one knows why, in singular contempt, along with Hungarian dance and generals." Every country estate was at that time a palace that, in addition to numerous servants, cooks, coachmen, nursemaids, cockroaches, and a lack of hygienic arrangements, almost always housed some parasites: poor relations, a type of gentleman or lady deprived of means and incapable of working, maintained by the landowner. They had in common an ostentatious love for the French language (which they thought brought them closer to the nobility), touchiness, and hatred for the peasants. "Gentlemen of easy temper," Dostoyevsky describes them, "capable of telling little stories, playing a game of cards, and decidedly opposed to tasks of whatever kind. . . ."

Foma Fomich—that is, Thomas the son of Thomas. Perhaps there is something comic, in Russian, in having the same name as one's father. Like the protagonist of Gogol's "Overcoat," Akaky Akakyevich, and so many of Bulgakov's characters, Filip Filipovich, Poligraf Poligrafovich, Ferapont Ferapontovich—all the way to Yevtushenko's Kompromis Kompromisovich.

"*Je suis un* simple parasite *et rien de plus!*" says Stepan Trofimovich, the celebrated parasite of *The Possessed*. According to him, "The Russian countryside, in a thousand years, has given us nothing but the dance of the *Kamarinski*"; agreeing, in this, with Foma Fomich, who defines that unbridled peasant dance, which inspired Glinka, as "the apotheosis of drunkenness."

One good memory of Stepan Trofimovich remains, in any case: two little verses that, during a railway journey, our parasite "kept stammering, following the sound of the train:

> Vek and Vck, and Lev Kambek
> Lev Kambek, and Vek and Vek."

The mystery in which the translator has left these verses renders them more attractive, and difficult to forget. Then (unfortunately) everything becomes clear: *Vek* (*The Century*) was the title of a review of that time, and

Lev (Leo) Kambek the name of an editor of reviews. Stepan Trofimovich had literary ambitions—like Foma Fomich, who wanted to "refine the customs" of the old servant Gavriil (Gabriel) by teaching him French.

⬳

Dostoyevsky liked to draw, as did Victor Hugo—who, along with George Sand, was Dostoyevsky's favorite among foreign writers—and the beloved Pushkin. While he was writing *Prestuplenie i Nakazanie* (*Crime and Punishment*), he drew the faces of his characters on the page. His favorite painting was Raphael's *Sistine Madonna,* in the art museum in Dresden. He stood for hours in front of this painting.

When he took pen in hand he often didn't know what he was going to write. "I have absolutely no idea how this novel will turn out," he said while working on *The Gambler* (completed in twenty-six days). Lack of money forced him to write in an inhuman manner: in a hurry, without being able to reread, make corrections—"under the whip."

He worked at night and got up at eleven.

When he began his first novel, *Poor Folk,* he had no

literary acquaintances except D. V. Grigorovich, who up to that point had written only one article: "The Hurdy-Gurdy Player of Petersburg."

Dostoyevsky was considered an author of outstanding serial novels. "A master of bad style," said Truman Capote. He wrote clichés without hesitation: "His teeth were like pearls, his lips of coral."

He deemed Levin the main character of *Anna Karenina.*

He loved eel, white Rhine wines, sweets (the Ballet pastry shop, in Petersburg, was his favorite).

He loved the cathedral of Milan, and punctuality: when he set a time for an appointment he always added, "Neither before nor after."

When he rode in a carriage he would talk to the coachman.

He wrote, "Or is it possible that man doesn't want well-being?"

☞

Tolstoy—which an acquaintance of the writer Ennio Flaiano pronounced as if it were a French name, Tolstwa—is not to be confused, of course, with Count Aleksei Tolstoy, the wealthiest Soviet writer.

According to Slonim, he "had even kept his old valet, who, as the story went in Moscow, used to answer the telephone: 'His Highness is at the Central Committee of the Communist Party.' "

The wooden house that Tolstoy bought in Moscow on Dolgo-Khamovnicheski (now Krapotkinskaya) Ulitsa, which today is the Tolstoy Museum, and one of the last wooden houses remaining in Moscow, did not have a bath. Instead of having one built, Tolstoy went once a week to the public baths. A foreign visitor reports that he smelled of cypress wood. (Similarly, the old servant of Lavretsky, in Turgenev's *Home of the Gentry,* standing behind his master's chair at dinnertime, spread around "a musty scent reminiscent of cypress wood.") Tolstoy had made his study in the basement, and he wrote by the light of a single candle. He did not wear glasses. When he was tired of writing sitting down, he moved his work to a high shelf and wrote standing, like Peter the Great. When he married, he no longer had any teeth. His cook had to make special dishes for him, different from those for the rest of the family and the guests. The cook was called Nikolai Mikhailovich and was a former flute player. He baked some excellent hot pastries, which he made rise by blowing air into them, not through a straw but directly with his mouth, as if he were playing the flute. They were called "sighs of Nikolai." When he died, he was succeeded by his son Semyon, who prepared for Tolstoy exclusively vegetarian dishes.

One has the idea that Tolstoy was born before Dostoyevsky, while in fact he was seven years younger: it was only that he aged more. Until the age of eighty he always went on horseback. His last horse was called Delirium. He knew horses better than anyone else. He spoke to them. He could read the tiredness in the eye of an old horse. He wrote the best story about a horse: "Kholstomer."

When he died, at Astapovo, the painter Leonid Pasternak came from Moscow to make a portrait of him. He brought along, as his assistant, his twenty-year-old son, Boris.

☞

The family of the last czar formed a handsome photographic group. Good-looking, elegant, clean, without bugs. Their intelligence—unfortunately, in a time when much was needed—was limited. The writer most admired by Empress Alexandra and her lady companions was, says Nabokov, Ella Wheeler Wilcox.

When their bones were found, it was seen that the family was not complete. The Czarevitch Alexis and the Grand Duchess Anastasia were missing. Beside the skeletons of the czar, the czarina, and their children were found others, among them that of a dog (certainly not called Sharik), who had faithfully followed his masters to Ekaterinburg, and that of their cook.

Perhaps, during the bitter time of imprisonment, the cook had tried to distract Nicholas II from the nightmare of the future by bringing him at table his favorite dish: roast suckling pig with horseradish sauce.

⌒

Badenweiler, Germany, Villa Friederike, July 2, 1904. Dr. Schwöhrer had a good idea: "He had a bottle of champagne brought up. Chekhov took the glass that was offered to him and said, 'It's been such a long time since I drank champagne.' He emptied the glass and lay on his side. After a little he breathed no more."

The Russians light a candle beside a person who is about to die. When death arrives they put out the candle. Even Dostoyevsky, foreseeing that moment, asked his wife to light a candle for him. On the eyes, closed forever, two five-kopeck pieces are placed. The dead person is laid not on a bed but on a table, which is closer than a bed to the idea the Russian has of sleeping, and then he is transported to the cemetery in an open casket. On returning from the cemetery the survivors refresh themselves by eating *kutya*—rice cooked with honey, crushed nuts, and raisins.

IV

I was born just in time to see the Russia of Chekhov. It was at the home of my paternal grandmother, in Sondrio, on the Piazzi Prospect, where my grandmother, who was a widow, lived, looked after by a servant (a serf) named Caterina, a good woman, more patient than a Russian with the capriciousness of her mistress, who was very proud of her aristocratic title. Caterina lived in the house as part of the family, without receiving any wages, like Lenchen, the faithful servant of Marx.

In the courtyard, where the stalls for the horses were and the coach houses and perhaps even a sleigh, lived another serf, of whom I remember only his nickname: Patato (probably not even he remembered his name or surname). Patato did whatever jobs his masters ordered him to do, contenting himself with bread and soup, an occasional glass of wine, some cast-off clothes, a space under the stairs where he slept, and a toilet that Frate Indovino would have called "very . . . Russian."

A story was told of Patato that once, in recompense for a job he had done, Caterina offered him a glass of Sassella wine, pouring it absentmindedly into a glass in which she had left an egg white. Patato drank the wine in a gulp, as was his custom, and gave back the glass with a strange expression of uncertainty on his face. Asked by Caterina if the wine was not good, he said, "It's sort of hard." A response become proverbial, which, now that he is dead, is all that remains of Patato on this earth.

*J*ourney
to the
Land of the Flies

(1 9 8 4)

I

Villa Musco at Spartà. The Milanese servant of Angelo Musco. Musco's matchboxes. The song of the fly. A gift to the czar. The handshake of the plumber. Ettore Majorana's hair. The public toilet of Lipari. The handshake of the public toilet's custodian.

I stayed for some time in the lovely Villa Musco, near the village of Spartà, in Sicily, not far from Messina. I had been given a beautiful bedroom, with great, transparent curtains at the windows which swelled slowly in the breeze filtering between the wooden slats of the open shutters and kept out the flies and mosquitoes that are seldom absent from earthly paradises. Gilded furniture gave the room a warm glow: it had once furnished the dressing room of the great villa that Angelo Musco, the famous Sicilian actor, had built in Catania, where he was born. Starting from nothing— or, rather, from less than nothing—he had arrived where he had arrived. He was a heavy smoker. Every morning, his Milanese servant, Tarenzi by name, set before him a new box of wax matches, which would last him for the day. Musco wrote the date on the box and initialed it, so that no one else would use it. At night the box ended up in one of the many little gilded drawers of the dressing room, adding to the hundreds of other boxes, all the same, that were kept there in meticulous order. In those days Messina exported—among other things—capers, maidenhair, liquorice root, bones, gunpowder; and from the nearby harbor of Riposto ships loaded with snow gathered on Etna departed for Malta. . . .

My room had a huge bathroom, with the hygienic apparatus widely scattered in the four corners and a window that looked onto a hip roof covered with tarpaper and enclosed by a little wall that from below made it look like a terrace. The sky, atop that black base, became even bluer.

The name Musco surely derives from *mosca* ("fly"; *musca* in Sicilian). Musco had some qualities in common with the fly: obstinacy, a sharp eye, rapidity of movement (when in flight, the fly beats its wings two hundred times a second), and even impudence, a characteristic of the fly that was first noted by the illustrious Sicilian scholar Baron Serafino Amabile Guastella.

In front of the villa is a big paved open space, with various armchairs adapted to the varied shapes of men and women, and an iron breakfast table: tea, coffee, milk, butter, citron marmalade, buttery biscuits (a specialty of Messina), and excellent toast. The crumbs are carefully gathered and given to the domestic animals to eat; if a piece of bread falls on the ground one picks it up and kisses it. So, at least, it used to be, when all the peasants ate together from the same plate or even directly off the marble table, onto which the pasta was dumped. The peasants said, *"Nun fari di pani Bartulumeo,"* that is, "Don't make a Saint Bartholomew of the bread," eating only the crust and leaving the white (the saint's skin was removed, as one can see from his statue in the cathedral of Milan). According to a legend related by Nabokov, Saint Bartholomew—perhaps the least known of the twelve apostles—"was flayed alive and exposed to the flies" at Albanopolis, today

Derbent, on the shore of the Caspian Sea, some two hundred kilometers north of Baku. His coffin, thrown into the sea, floated miraculously all the way to the island of Lipari, not far from Messina, where his name became Bartulumeo.

After dinner we went to sit in front of the house, chatting, smoking, dozing, meditating on the more extraordinary dishes brought that day to the table, as they do in the Sicilian nobles' clubs. The sun shone gently on the lion-colored earth of the flower beds and among the hundred different greens of the plants, all evergreen: cedars of Lebanon, palms, eucalyptus, pines, silver firs, figs, a pepper tree (false pepper) attacked by ivy, olives, carob trees, holm oaks; and myrtle, rosemary, asparagus, bamboo, oleander, mimosa, hibiscus, jasmine, and capers, which are flowers, like jasmine, or, more precisely, edible flowers, like cauliflower and artichokes.

Certainly some names are missing from that list. The only plant with deciduous leaves grows behind the villa. It is a mulberry—nearly as immense as the beeches of the Valle del Bove (Valley of the Ox) on Etna—which makes the row of huts for the caretakers, the peasants, and the tanks of potable water seem tiny. On the low wall that forms a boundary of the kitchen garden, at a fly's flight from the kitchen, Sicilian basil, with small leaves, grows in a big terra-cotta vase—the basil that, as the peasants teach, must be watered at night. A buzzing fly grazes my ear.

"The peasants"—again Baron Serafino Amabile Guastella intervenes—"call animals by the names of their patron saints. They call horses Giorgio, asses Erasmo, mules Eligio, pigs Antonio, oxen Luca, wolves Silvestro." And the fly? The fly is called simply "fly," because, fortunately for us, it doesn't have a patron saint. And not having a patron saint, it has to protect itself, sharpening its wits. Exactly as Musco did.

Having reluctantly tried various careers, he realized that he was born to fly in a theater, and he finally succeeded in climbing onto a stage. His war-horse was "The Song of the Fly," which quickly became so popular that he himself was nicknamed "'a Musca" (the Fly), and no one knew that his real name was Musco.

Street of the Land of the Flies is one of the many streets in Palermo's Vucciria (from the French *boucherie*), the quarter where the old food market was. Another street is called Street of the Flying Chairs. Small shops with the sign BROTH AND MEAT sell *quarume,* a stew made from the less noble parts of the steer. *Stigghiole* are lamb entrails roasted on a spit with onions and parsley: azure smoke and an exquisite aroma. Bright lights illuminate the fish (tunafish with red carnations in their mouths) and make their scales sparkle.

At the entrance to the Vucciria there were once boys who, for payment, at a nod from a shopper, would line up behind him (it has always been men who do the shopping) and carry his bag—which became ever heavier with the accumulation of purchases—and, when he had finished, carry it to his house.

Musco, who was his mother's twenty-third child, learned to read and write at the age of twenty-six. The celebrated Grasso-Musco theater company made a world tour: Argentina, Spain, France, Germany, Hungary, Russia. The czar went to see it. He understood, as everyone did, what the actors were reciting in Sicilian; he enjoyed himself and invited them to the Kremlin. After giving Grasso a gold snuffbox, he had a parchment brought in on which the names of the actors had been written in illuminated letters, and asked them all to sign it. Giovanni Grasso signed first. None of the other actors in the company knew how to write, and each signed with a cross. Musco overcame the humiliation of the moment with the impudence of the fly. He said, "To the poor czar we give a cemetery."

The conversation after lunch is interrupted by the plumber, who, having finished repairing a faucet, comes out of the house and, before starting for the gate, ceremoniously shakes hands with everyone.

☞

Leaving Messina the car had skirted the little lakes of Ganzirri—'u Pantanu (the quagmire) and 'u Pantaneddu (the little quagmire)—surrounded by tiny cottages, wooden huts, stands selling clams and eels, fishermen, small trattorias; it climbed among the olives, leaving below the green sea, and suddenly I found myself in the garden of the villa. Entering the house, I glimpsed in the semidarkness the great dining room, with its long, long table. . . . In other words: the exquisite dishes of the colorful Sicilian cuisine . . . every day . . . keeping alive the admonishing memory of what happened to Dionysus the Elder, tyrant of Syracuse.

In 367 B.C., with the tragedy *The Ransom of Hector,* performed in Athens, Dionysus won a literary prize and, like a good Sicilian, wished to celebrate the event with a banquet. I don't know if, like his fellow citizen Charmos, he kept at hand, while he ate, verses of Homer and Euripides and proverbs to cite in relation to every dish that was placed before him; but as for the food, it is probable that he regulated himself according to the ancient equivalent of the Sicilian saying "There is always room for an unexpected mouthful." As often happens with tyrants, he exaggerated. He died at table, where one can put off old age but not death. (Nor did his tragedy survive him; already judged mediocre by contemporaries, it confirms that even in antiquity literary prizes tended to be awarded to mediocre works.)

Two very special dishes have, by force of circumstance, eluded me: *stigghiole,* seen only from a distance on a street in Messina (as I was passing in a car, with no possibility of stopping, I saw the unmistakable azure smoke); and *scuma* (foam), the finest spaghetti, thinner than angel hair, a specialty of Catania, the city of the great physicist Ettore Majorana, who let his hair grow very long, like a generous portion of *scuma,* in order not to waste precious time at the barber's. As the young Stendhal did, too.

In the piazza in Lipari, on the island of capers and Saint Bartulumeo, the first thing that catches the eye is a sign with a big arrow over the word "Toilets." The public toilet is built underground. One descends a wide—I was about to say monumental—staircase open to the sky and arrives at the custodian, a noble old man who sits smoking at a tottering little table at the entrance to his subterranean residence. On the table is an empty coffee cup, a full ashtray, and a plate with some change on it: the collection plate.

He confirms that Filippino (up on the piazza) is the best restaurant: "Even the flies know it!"

"Is it expensive?"

"Depends on what you eat. Tomorrow, the sixteenth of September," he announces, "the public toilets will close."

"Damn," I cannot help saying, "and where will people go . . . ?"

The answer is a vague gesture.

I glance up at the sky of Lipari, so beautiful as seen from the depths of the public toilet, and suddenly I remember the toilet in the public garden beside the lake in Zurich: a kind of chalet, or, rather, a lakeside temple—clean, odorless, with hot water, soft paper towels, receptacle for used towels, mirror, coat hook, Thonet chair . . .

Certainly, there are some differences between the toilet in Zurich and the one on the island of capers. Nevertheless, an imaginary thread connects the two constructions—one aboveground, the other underground—situated a thousand kilometers from each other: they belong to the same family.

Leaving, I gratefully place my bit on the collection plate. The noble old man rises, with difficulty, and ceremoniously shakes my hand.

"Here," he says, "one would stay very happily, except that every so often some boy throws down a rock."

II

The nocturnal appearance of Musco. My father's matchboxes. His library. End of a hunter's career. The penduline bird. Heraclitus the Obscure. The Heraclitus of San Simpliciano. Night on the Strait. The polar star. Aunt Anna's *riso in bianco*.

When I woke the morning after my arrival, the villa was immersed in silence. Seeping through the shutters, the dawn light reawakened the gold of the furniture, and perhaps the soul of poor Tarenzi. The previous night, after dinner, Musco had been evoked by his son and daughters, called up on the television screen in the clothes of the old professor of Pirandello's *Think It Over, Giacomino!*, who is described thus: "He is a poor old man of seventy, who can barely hold himself on his legs." Musco had improved this stage direction with an incredible disjointed gait, probably a memory of when, as a boy, he had tried to learn the art of resoling old shoes, working under the guidance of a master cobbler. It's well known that these masters are often confined to their benches by motor difficulties. I saw the son and the two daughters watching and listening intently: automatically their mouths murmured lines that they knew by heart, and I envied them this possibility of evoking their father in his house.

My father, too, who lived obscurely, like so many— infinitely many—others, was, like Musco, a great consumer of wax matches. He smoked Toscano cigars and always held between his blackened teeth a stub that threatened to go out at any moment. Often, lighting a wax match while he was talking, he would go on talking and forget that he had lighted it until the flame burned his fingers. I see him shaking his hand to put out the flame and then, instead of throwing the match away or putting it in the ashtray, making it disappear into the box, under the little sliding drawer of that ingenious container. At home, next to the red velvet armchair where he sat after dinner to read and smoke, he had a little table he had built himself which answered all his needs. On top, on a circular shelf, there was a lamp with a red silk shade that spread over our evenings a vaguely infernal light. Below, on a second, square shelf, the necessities for smoking: the box of cigars, the ashtray—too small, as Italian ashtrays usually are—and a box of matches that my mother (there was a little of Tarenzi in our house as well) replaced with a new one when it was almost empty. (The empty box ended up not in a gilded drawer but in the kitchen.) The cigar box was of pewter, lined, like a Havana-cigar box, with thin strips of exotic wood impregnated with the exquisite aroma of the cigars, and had a cover decorated with a colored print under glass reproducing an English racehorse mounted by a tiny jockey. Finally, on the last shelf was the library, made up of four volumes: a treatise on inorganic chemistry, written by his uncle Tullio, who had been his teacher; the poetry and prose of Giosuè Carducci (then our national poet) in a beautiful edition; and the poems of the Milanese Carlo Porta. When Papa was holding the Porta, he would every so often read some verses aloud to us.

The pages of the Carducci were folded and creased,

covered with pencil marks and fingerprints, which at the time annoyed me but which demonstrated the enthusiasm and also the judgment of the reader, who, like many of his generation, was an ardent follower of Carducci. When the poet died, Papa took the train to Bologna for his funeral, mixing with a crowd that came from all over Italy. And of that out-of-the-ordinary day, and also of that expense, he was always proud. Being from the mountains of Valtellina, he was a passionate hunter, and as a target shooter he had won many gold medals, which the hardships of life had obliged him gradually to sell. But his career as a hunter ended quite early, in the final glance of a chamois fatally wounded. He sold his gun and kept only his hunting knife, with its handle of deer horn, which he used as a paper cutter. As I do today.

⌒

I went out of the room trying not to make any noise and, descending a beautiful grand staircase with broad stone steps, reached the ground floor and went to sit outside at the breakfast table, still unset, to wait for the house to wake up, and even—who knows?—for poor Tarenzi, called up by the nocturnal appearance of his master, to come and put down on the table the breakfast tray with the new box of wax matches on it.

A black cat climbed cautiously up the leaning trunk of a palm from whose top hung, attached by a cord of woven grass and oscillating in every least breath of wind, the flask-shaped nest of a hanging bird, *Anthoscopus* ("explorer of flowers") *pendulinus*. Above the green of the plants the dome of the sky was blue, not the vulgar azure of postcards but as if Goya himself had painted it, and behind the blue of the sky I seemed to glimpse something obscurely clear, as when Heraclitus says that the sun has the width of the human foot.

The maidservant appeared. A gentle face, a nice white apron over a work dress of pale blue, a color repulsive to flies but not to man—the ideal person to make a house comfortable.

Heraclitus was nicknamed the Obscure because he wrote in a way that could be read only by the very few capable of understanding him: if he seems clear, as in the case of the diameter of the sun, one must suspect that he is being even more obscure than usual. When he could no longer endure the "clarity" of his fellow citizens he retired to the mountains, feeding, like a hermit, on grasses and wild greens. He became sick with dropsy. He returned to the city, where, stretching out on the ground, he had himself covered with manure so that the heat of the fermentation would dry him out. After two days of this cure he died. Neanthes of Cyzicum adds that having lost, under the manure, every human semblance, he was devoured by dogs. He was also nicknamed the weeping philosopher, as opposed to Democritus, the laughing philosopher.

Many years later, Carlo Emilio Gadda called himself "the twisted Heraclitus of Via San Simpliciano" (where he lived). Instead of retiring to the wild mountains of Asia Minor, Gadda retired to the seven hills of Rome, where he lived on fettuccine, artichokes *alla romana,* etc. But the sadness was the same.

☙

When I left Sicily, it was night on the Strait of Messina. In the deep darkness only the lights of the harbor were visible, and the smaller ones of Villa San Giovanni, and the very distant ones of Reggio-Calabria. An infinity of stars sparkled in the black sky, and among them I recognized, at the end of the constellation Ursa Minor, the little Polar Star, which for Sicilians marks the mythic

North, and which had guided the long, laborious march of an obscure Sicilian actor from his island up and up to success in Milan. From the light of that star all the rest was derived—the villa, the garden, the room with its gilded furnishings, the long dining table . . .

Orsa Minore is also the name of a restaurant in East Hampton, New York, owned by a Sicilian cook (that's why I remember it), who studied cooking and worked in Switzerland, in the canton of Ticino. His specialty: tortelloni with mushroom sauce, a dish more Ticinese than Sicilian. One day I stopped the car in front of his restaurant. I wanted to ask him why he had given it that name. But the season was over and the restaurant was closed. In an astronomy book I read that the constellation in which the Greeks, poetically, saw a bear and the Romans, more practical, a chariot seemed to the Chinese, more cooking-minded, a frying pan.

Back on the Continent, I had a desire for a plate of *riso in bianco* as I had eaten it as a child in Florence, at my dear aunt Anna's house, Villa Torriccia. At the gate of the villa was the concierges' house (they used to call me "signorino") and at the back of the garden was another structure, a sort of cottage used as the garage, with an apartment for the driver above. (Later, in less easy times, it was rented to a painter.) The cook was from Greve, a little town in Chianti, and her name was Assunta. She was illiterate, which was at that time quite common—one of so many people who lived their entire lives without reading a line—but in Tuscan cooking, although she could not consult Artusi's famous cookbook, she was very skilled. Around the dinner table there were always a lot of us, as at Spartà, so the rice arrived on an immense platter that Assunta had a hard time holding. My uncle, at the head of the table, was the first to be served. He was the master. He tasted a mouthful and nodded to Assunta, authorizing her to serve the others. When, later, the chicken arrived at the table, after a taste my uncle would say—as if obliged by the chicken itself, which for its sacrifice seemed to demand a word of appreciative recognition—"Chicken is always chicken."

The *riso in bianco* was neither a Tuscan dish nor a complicated one: large-grain rice, well cooked but not overcooked, and seasoned with a lot of fresh butter and grated Parmesan. It was absolutely white, with shades of light azure, and very good. Perhaps it depended on the quality of the rice. Perhaps on the butter or the Parmesan. Perhaps Assunta had a secret. I have tried several times to make it but have never succeeded in getting the same delicacy.

Another characteristic of that rice is this: all who then sat gaily around the table before their plates of rice (Alex, the younger son of my aunt and uncle—thin, with a big Adam's apple, characteristics of a heavy eater—used to take an enormous helping) are, except for the writer, dead. Even Assunta, the cook, who ended her days in Sesto San Giovanni, near Milan, a place without hills, without vines, without olive trees, without cypresses, without laurels. And even the lovely Villa Torriccia, demolished to make room for condominiums.

Says Heraclitus the Obscure, "The living and the dead, the waked and the sleeper, are the same."

*T*ravels to Djakarta, Gorgonzola, Crescenzago, London, Milan

(1 9 6 3 – 8 3)

I

Beautiful feet. Love sacred and profane. The mother-of-pearl button. Rossini. The train and the interior monologue. Radio Peking. The tourist tour of Gorgonzola. Curnonsky. The invention of Gorgonzola. The beautiful young waitress of Crescenzago.

*Y*ears ago I found myself in Indonesia, in Djakarta, which was once called Batavia, sitting at a table in a restaurant in the heart of the Chinese quarter of Glodok—near Kota, to anyone who knows this city, immense in extent, where the long streets change their names every two or three blocks, causing the visitor to go mad. I was reflecting on the menu, undecided between serpent soup, roast monkey, or a simple stuffed dog with hot pepper.

A young woman sitting at the next table with some other people was showing off her beautiful feet, at once thin and soft, brown on top and pink underneath, on which no shoe had left the slightest mark. In Indonesia feet are considered the most fascinating part of the female body, and everyone knows what small female feet mean to the Japanese; it is also known that in Vienna, around 1910, the tram stops were always crowded with groups of gentlemen waiting to admire the small feet of pretty women poking out from under their skirts for an instant as they boarded the car.

I myself have always had a weakness for women's feet, and I hate people who tell jokes in which feet are associated with the odor of certain cheeses, like Appenzeller, Camembert, Gorgonzola. For these same people, armpits can smell only of goats, and the . . .

"It," a sommelier would say, "has an intoxicating bouquet of roses and Parma violets. . . ." I would add that "it," because of its form—rounder than any solid of revolution or any circle traced by a compass—and because of its inscrutable mixture of the human and the divine, can be considered one of the most convincing proofs of the existence of God, certainly more convincing than the ontological argument of Saint Anselm.

And yet how long has the misunderstanding of the two kinds of love, the sacred and the profane, lasted, a misunderstanding that has confused the minds of countless poor devils and she-devils? I remember an old lady who boasted of having never shown herself naked to her husband. Asked how she had conceived her numerous children, she answered that she had a nightgown with a little flap in the front, usually fastened by a mother-of-pearl button, through which . . .

Thus she lived (with a husband worthy of her in every way) and died, convinced that she had followed the road of virtue that leads directly to paradise, which, if it is inhabited by similar angels, is nothing but the inferno—rather, the worst inferno, because it is not that of the lustful, the gluttonous, the prodigal, the miserly, the wrathful, the slothful, the heretic, the unbeliever, the violent, the fraudulent, or the betrayer but the most horrible of all: the inferno of the idiot.

A friend, after reading these last lines (the nightgown with the flap), told me that a similar story, though without the mother-of-pearl button, is found in a book of Carlo Dossi's. This seems yet another confirmation of the fact that by now everything has been written and the writer of today can add of his own at most a mother-of-pearl button; and often he does not add even that. . . .

From Milan the train travels silently toward Gorgonzola through a green plain divided geometrically by canals full of clear water, with granite locks. Rows of enormous poplars with dancing leaves (*Populus tremula*) lead to villas and farmhouses of splendid design, all destined to be covered in a few years with cement. And then the day will come when there will be a lack of good arable land, and all that cement will have to be removed, at enormous expense, in order that the earth underneath may be found again: in order to eat, to survive. As the train passes, large herds of cows with clean, fragrant coats look straight into my eyes without ceasing to chew their cud, as is their habit. Probably they are thinking the same thing. To Liszt, who had come to visit him, the old Rossini said he had composed some rather tasty little piano pieces, and had titled them "Fresh Butter," "Lentils," "Peas," "Macaroni" . . .

The interior monologue was born on a train. Joyce, rather than inventing it, perhaps used it excessively. It seems to me that Joyce took a route opposite to that of a normal writer: he began with a classic (*Dubliners*), continued with writings that became more and more complicated (*Portrait of the Artist, Ulysses*), and ended with a novel (*Finnegans Wake*) that is untranslatable and practically unreadable. Even if it's true that defects are an integral part of perfection, I would like to try eliminating part of *Ulysses*—pages that are more or less incomprehensible, plays on words, on style, on punctuation, things still taken up, unfortunately, by the last Joyceans—and see what happens.

One of the first stations is Crescenzago. In Crescenzago there was a little restaurant with a beautiful young waitress. . . . So, even if you discard a few pages . . . Many of Joyce's admirers might have had the same thought, but . . . But again the beautiful Indonesian woman comes back to my mind. To hell with serpents, monkeys, and dogs. I decided to order the same dish they served her, and when they brought her some spring rolls, I—instead of writing the order on the appropriate pad, which is on every table—simply pointed out the dish to the waiter. Of course, to point I used my thumb and not my index finger—to point with the index finger is considered a serious offense there—and I used my right hand because the left is considered dirty, being used for post-defecatory ablutions: toilet paper is unknown in the toilets there. I thought once of the embarrassing situations in which a beautiful left-handed girl might find herself; but surely I was mistaken, because tradition is always stronger than anything.

Meanwhile, various tour buses had stopped in front of the restaurant, and a crowd of hot tourists had invaded the place. An infinity of feet—deformed by shoes and by calluses of every sort, and by twisted nails painted in lively colors to attract attention to their deformity (feet that irresistibly evoked the most vulgar jokes)—and dozens of buttocks that could testify only to the existence of the devil noisily found seats at the tables. The proprietor, one of the seven million Chinese with the family name Chang, turned up the volume on the speakers in honor of the guests. In addition to the eternal "The Orient Is Red," the most recent successful songs were being transmitted from Peking: "Recover the Losses Caused by the Four" and "Govern the State Centering the Work on the Class Struggle."

☞

At the tourist office in Gorgonzola I take a leaflet with a plan for the tour of the city: photographic safari in the public park, which is inhabited by dwarf goats, hens, cockerels, pigeons, pheasants, swans, guinea pigs, ponies, donkeys. Then a stop at the ancient bakery on the Martesana canal and consumption on the spot of a fresh, ring-shaped loaf of French bread. After the ancient bakery, a visit to the terra-cotta kitchenware workshops, with shopping; a visit to a cheese factory (as in London one might visit a brewery), with, at the end, a taste of Gorgonzola accompanied by a little glass of sweet wine, offered by the firm as an aperitif. Finally comes lunch at the ancient inn where Renzo, the humble hero of Manzoni's great novel *The Betrothed*, fleeing Milan, stopped for dinner, and where the seat he occupied (nearest the entrance, "the place for the bashful," says Manzoni) is marked by a plaque on the wall— just like the place reserved for Curnonsky in so many restaurants in Paris and the rest of France, where the celebrated prince of gastronomes could sit and eat, free, whatever he wanted.

After lunch, to complete the tour, there remain two monuments to photograph: the chapel in the middle of the Piazza della Chiesa dedicated to Saints Sebastian and Rocco, which was erected by Saint Carlo Borromeo during the plague of 1577; and, behind the church, the beautiful ancient bell tower, at the top of which Bishop

Ottone Visconti hid, after losing the battle of Gorgonzola (1278), and thus saved his life.

It is true that Curnonsky could sit and eat whatever he wanted free, but it must be said that in his last years, just when these plaques became so widespread, he was constrained to live on milk alone.

Normally Curnonsky would have a good meal at midday, and at night, for dinner, a hard-boiled egg. His name was Maurice Edmond Sailland, and by his friends he was called Cur, or Curne. From his youth he had had literary ambitions, while his father wanted to start him in trade. Why, the young Maurice asked himself, should I not write? Why not? *Cur non* (in Latin)? This was the modest origin of his curious pen name, completed with a Russian ending, in homage to the fashion of those days, which originated with the czar's visit to Paris. After working as a ghostwriter for Willy, Colette's first husband, he turned finally to gastronomy, with what success everyone knows. He died at eighty-three, when he fell off a balcony; and perhaps, flying down toward the pavement of the courtyard, he was thinking, for the last time: Why not?

Gorgonzola, I am told, was invented by chance in the last century by Signor Vergani, yet in the Piazza della Chiesa there is no monument representing him in the act of making the fortunate mistake in his work. This unintentional birth has nothing embarrassing about it; rather, it unites Gorgonzola with other classic delights of gastronomy, such as (to give a single example) chicken Marengo, which was improvised, with the means at hand on the battlefield, by Napoleon's Swiss chef: a chicken destined (perhaps) to live longer than the memory of the battle itself, and—destiny is strange—created for a man who, in addition to the many faults of which Madame de Staël accuses him, had the unpardonable one of considering time spent at the table time lost.

Gorgonzola has established (it seems) a twinship with Stilton, the English city that gives its name to the cheese with blue mold which is quite similar to Gorgonzola and is served with a piece of crusty bread and a glass of port. Today the production of Stilton is threatened by an enormous coal bed that has been discovered just beneath the land where the cheese is produced. The land of Gorgonzola doesn't have coal beds, but in any case they would not be a threat, because Gorgonzola— and here is the most startling information—is now made not in Gorgonzola yet in Novara, in Piedmont.

Other modifications to the tour of the city:

The terra-cotta workshops: they don't exist any longer.

The Manzonian inn: where it was there is today a furniture store.

The chapel of San Carlo: it stood until the end of the eighteenth century; then nothing more is known of it.

The bell tower: it was demolished a century and a half ago, when the new church was built. What is Gorgonzola today, without Gorgonzola, without the ancient bell tower, without the Manzonian inn, without the chapel of San Carlo Borromeo, without the terra-cotta workshops, without a monument to Signor Vergani?

Is it nothing? Is it just a place like so many others, a place where everything there was to see has been destroyed or taken away?

Maybe so. And yet, I think—on the train returning to Milan, and assailed again by the temptation to interior monologue—it is nevertheless worth the trouble to go to Gorgonzola, even if only for the animals in the park, for passing through Crescenzago, for the lack of tourists, for the taste, on the still and silent banks of the Martesana, of the fresh French ring bread, which comes out of the oven at eleven, as I recall. . . . Men and women could be divided into two categories: those who can wear a watch on their wrist, and those who cannot, because the watch hangs crooked, with the back of the face hitting the bone. . . . Yes, it's worthwhile to go to Gorgonzola if only to pass through Crescenzago.

The beautiful waitress of Crescenzago had the whitest skin, lightly rosy on her cheeks, whose fragrance was the sum of all the natural perfumes emanating from a lovely female body—among them, besides the already mentioned scent of roses and Parma violets, the scent of vanilla cake, of the bosom (except for the bosom of Joan of Aragon, the queen of Castile, which smelled of ripe peaches), the Paradise perfume of the mouth, and so on.

Perhaps someone may wish to know something more. How she looked: blonde or brunette, the eyes, the mouth; tall, medium, short, plump; hands, feet . . . But physical descriptions, good for passports, are useless in a narrative work. Better, then, to point to some particular more indirect: she had a childish smile without being childish, her flesh was firm and yet soft, she appeared tall or short according to the moment, her feet were equal to her hands. The sight of this enchanting girl, while with one knee next to her cheek she was attending to the toenails of one foot, was, as the Michelin guide says, worth not only a detour but a journey of its own.

II

Joan the Mad. The beauty of the Grand Duke of Virginia. The siege of Paris. The bell dinner and the Sun King. Dinner at the Trattoria del Nonno. Pepper not freshly ground. The beneficial effect of wine. Zeno of Citium and Zeno of Elea.

Joan of Aragon was very beautiful. Her bosom, as I just said, had the fragrance of ripe peaches, a quality that even today has never been attributed to any other woman. The king, Philip the Fair, at first was stunned by that fragrance. Then, probably, he got used to it. Joan was desperately in love with him and extremely jealous; upset by his betrayals, she developed a morbid melancholy that soon became madness. Philip had her shut up in the castle of Tordesillas, where she remained a prisoner for many years. When Philip the Fair finally died, Joan for a long time did not want to be separated from his coffin. Her subjects called her Juana la Loca—

Joan the Mad. Thus she became one of that group of historical personages—among them her husband, Philip the Fair, Pépin the Short, Henry the Fowler, John Lackland (brother of Richard the Lion-Hearted)—whose nicknames canceled out all other aspects of their personalities.

The kings of Aragon were rich in nicknames. Besides the usual ones dictated by the adulatory rhetoric of the courtiers—the Catholic, the Magnanimous, the Just, the Great, the Conqueror—I find Henry the Sickly, Peter the Ceremonious, Alfonso the Kind, and Alfonso the Chaste. Among them Joan would have felt ill at ease, embarrassed by rather than proud of her perfume, which today, with fruit that ripens in the refrigerator, would seem even more intoxicating. A portrait of her in the Louvre is attributed to Raphael; it seems, however, that he did not actually see her, since, he says, he sent an assistant to Naples to paint her face from life. But the idea of the portrait was his. Her bosom, as far as one can tell from the little that is visible above the bodice's embroidered edges, fastened with a jewel, seems more compact and abundant than that of La Fornarina, which, fortunately, is visible. Philip the Fair, like Dr. Bovary, perhaps failed to comprehend: he found himself before "*une femme en toilette fine, charmante et sentant frais, à ne savoir même d'où venait cette odeur, ou si ce n'était pas sa peau qui parfumait sa chemise.*"

Anyone who, visiting the Louvre, finds himself before the portrait is struck by Joan's gaze, which fixes him intensely (as in Naples she must have fixed her gaze on the painter's eyes), as if she wished to confide something to him, perhaps the secret of her fragrance.

Another portrait of Joan, by an unknown painter, is in the Royal Academy of Arts in London. Here, too, she is beautiful, with a dreamy look that immediately draws one in, her bosom enclosed in a rigid corset that seems to guard the perfume.

While I stood there looking, fascinated, and with the sensation that the mystery was finally going to be cleared up, the guard, of whom until that moment I had taken no notice, broke the enchanted silence, saying: "Closing time, ladies and gentlemen."

Going out of the Royal Academy into Piccadilly, I walked along Duke Street and turned immediately into Jermyn Street, heading toward the shop of the famous perfumer Floris. I wanted to ask if there exists, or ever had existed, a perfume of ripe peaches. But then I let it go.

The vein of madness that runs in the Spanish branch of the Hapsburgs goes back to Joan of Aragon; and perhaps it is also in those who look at her too intensely.

☙

I return for a moment to what I was saying about the beautiful girl of Crescenzago—that is, to the best way of describing a person. The meticulous enumeration of physical characteristics, used so much in bad novels, serves no purpose. Every new characteristic, rather than blending with the preceding ones and little by little completing the portrait, cancels them, so to speak, and increases the fog that forms between the page and the reader. On the other hand: when Gide says of Claudel, "As a young man he had the look of a nail; now he seems a pestle," Claudel is immediately present, vivid, even though we do not know if he is tall or short, or what color his eyes are.

Lautréamont describes the beauty of the Grand Duke of Virginia thus: "Handsome as a dissertation on the curve that a dog describes running toward its master."

Lautréamont died very young, on November 24, 1870, in Paris, while the city was besieged by the Prussian army. Like nearly all the rest of the population, he must have suffered severe hunger—which is difficult to believe, since one instinctively thinks of Paris as an immense agglomeration of good restaurants. "It's no longer horsemeat that we're eating," Victor Hugo wrote in his diary; he was among the besieged, but certainly in better conditions than Lautréamont. "Perhaps dogmeat? Perhaps mouse?"

Paris had seen worse, and anyway the gastronomic talent of the Parisians did not fail even in the most atrocious circumstances. In 1617 the Maréchal d'Ancre, much hated by the people, was assassinated. The day after the assassination, his body was exhumed and cut in pieces by a savage crowd, which the day before had not been able to vent its hatred thoroughly. One of these "posthumous executioners" tore the heart out of the Maréchal's chest, intending to devour it in front of everyone. But before he brought it to his mouth he had it cooked *à point* over a charcoal fire, and sprinkled it with aromatic vinegar.

☞

Not many years later, in the time of the Sun King, the *souper à sonnette* was invented—the "bell dinner," during which the ladies sat at the table dressed only in powder, perfume, and jewels. On the backs of their chairs hung loose robes, to put on whenever the servants, summoned by the bell, entered to perform their duties. No servant of the time has left a memoir that might enable us to understand what thoughts passed through his mind while he was serving, for example, *côtelettes de mouton en papillotes*—a creation of the Marquise de Maintenon, who, according to someone, had made these dinners fashionable. Perhaps the most aphrodisiac effect was reserved precisely for the servants; and perhaps in the silvery sound of the bell one can discern the first signs of the future revolution.

Seen close up, the Sun King was less radiant than one would think. He had two teeth when he was born, but when he was a little over twenty he had to have all his teeth extracted by the court surgeon, because of an illness. There are various accounts of this matter: some say all, some many, some one. (His father, Louis XIII, on the other hand, had forty-eight teeth instead of the usual thirty-two.) In any case, the operation was not a success; the King lost a piece of his palate, and during meals bits of food often came out of his nose, which etiquette did not permit his fellow diners to notice. The

King, for his part, would have liked to eat alone, but not even he could escape the etiquette that prescribed his presence at table.

It is for this reason that when I sit in my place at the Trattoria del Nonno (not marked by any plaque or sign on the wall) and open the red plastic folder and scan the typewritten menu passing over all its usual errors and see so many dishes crossed off because they have run out among them just the one I was intending to have and at the same time feel a draft of cold air entering from the street together with a customer nicknamed Concorde because of the shape of his nose who goes and sits at the "family table" where the barber is holding forth . . . it is for this reason, as I was saying, that to recover my serenity it is enough to think for a moment of a banquet at the Court of the Sun King in the royal palace of Versailles.

Having finished the soup I ask for a glass of white wine. Then, since the wine and the soup were excellent, some meatballs.

"How many?"

"One."

It would be difficult in another place to order this way—to invent a meal as one is eating, according to one's appetite, even inverting the traditional order of the courses. Victor Hugo recounts that the actor Frédérick Lemaître would gladly have fish as the last course: "If he has turbot, he wants it served after the custard."

Having finished the meatball, I order two more of them, on which I sprinkle a generous knifepoint of gray pepper.

Here gastronomes will curl their lips. For them the word "pepper" must always be preceded by "freshly ground." But we must admit that there also exists pepper ground some time ago: it rules over innumerable tables in more modest establishments that lack pepper mills—they would be "freshly stolen"—and has a particular taste, different from that of freshly ground black or white pepper (doubtless very good), a taste, however, that I like, and I believe I am not the only one who likes it.

Having finished the meatballs, I order another glass of fresh white wine, which invites meditation. The beneficial effect of wine on the drinker has never been described so well as by Zeno of Citium, according to what Galen wrote in "The Faculties of the Soul Follow the Temperament of the Body," which is reported with great elegance by Giuseppe Averani in one of his most erudite lessons: "Zeno, as the founder of the austere and rigid Stoic doctrine, a man by profession harsh and rough and bitter, used to compare himself to *lupini:* just as *lupini*, when they are soaked, soften and sweeten, so he, drinking and plunging into the glasses, his native harshness and bitterness laid aside."

Zeno of Citium should not be confused with Zeno of Elea, a disciple of Parmenides, considered by Aristotle the inventor of logic ("cruel Zeno," Valéry calls him), and remembered above all as the inventor of the celebrated race between Achilles and the tortoise (one of his four paradoxical proofs against motion), in which, as everyone knows, swift-footed Achilles cannot succeed in catching the slow tortoise, who has departed with a small advantage.

First Travels

(1 9 3 9 – 6 3)

I

The hour when authoresses dip their pens in the inkwell. The Countess Hahn-Hahn courageously invites me to write. The grave of the dog Russ at Bayreuth. The Bar del Grillo and the four Cavazza sisters.

It was the hour when authoresses dip their pens in the inkwell. "One eye," says Heine, "looks at the paper and the other at an ordinary man: thus do all authoresses, with the exception of the Countess Hahn-Hahn, who has only one eye."

It was the hour when the horse—with its body firmly supported on its four hoofs while the tail, moving of its own accord, keeps the flies off—thinks twice as much as a normal man.

It was the hour when Saul Steinberg, in his room over the Bar del Grillo, says, "Picasso is only one of my precursors."

The sky had grown dark. Impelled by hunger we went into the dairy.

"This is the hour," someone said while the dairyman was putting the risotto on the table, "when it is forbidden to say Dantesque, Michelangelesque."

The stupor did not take away our appetites. When the meal was finished, cigarettes were lighted.

It was the hour when (many years ago) the Athenians, Herodotus says, "having dined, devoted themselves to sleep or to dice."

Not very exciting. We went to the movies. When the show was over I went to my room.

Sitting at the table I looked at the sheet of white paper in the circle of lamplight, like a ring into which I had to jump. At a certain point I brought my hand near the pen, but I did not dare to take it up . . . and finally, having sent everything to hell, I lay down in bed and turned out the light.

The lamp lost its luminosity but not all at once. For an instant it became greenish, like a phosphorescent ectoplasm, then disappeared. In the darkness I saw the Countess Hahn-Hahn, who, despite the absence of one eye, courageously dipped her pen in the inkwell and wrote. Was she an invention of Heine or did she truly exist? Only many years after that nocturnal apparition did I read that the owner of the dog Russ ("Soot"), buried at Bayreuth next to Wagner's tomb—that is, Wagner himself—had known, in 1843, in Dresden, where he was the royal master of the chapel, Maria von Konneritz, born Frik, a friend of the Countess Hahn-Hahn.

🙢

This beginning of the First Travels goes back several years. Today no one, if he must write, dips his pen in an inkwell; and no one, or almost no one, has the opportunity of observing a horse anymore. The Grillo ("cricket") was the hangout for students from the nearby Polytechnic and from the Architecture School of Milan. Pleasantly furnished by four young architects in the colors of a parrot, and run with a firm hand by the four Cavazza sisters, at night it was the only light shining in the darkness of Via Pascoli, shining even through fog. On the second floor were some rooms, in the rear a little garden, with a dance floor; the food, like that of certain questionable inns of Pigalle, in Paris, was excellent. "Maria, the cook," Steinberg recalls, "was very fat, and always stayed in the kitchen.

Through the little window that gave onto the restaurant from the kitchen, one saw only a fragment of her—large white face; three, four chins. Her features were concentrated in the center of her face, leaving big empty spaces. Father Cavazza was always sitting in the courtyard, where at night the dancing took place. He was a handsome, dignified old man, a Roman senator, who, translated into a woman, was disastrous. Luigi, the waiter, wore tails. His gray hair, stuck down with gum, looked like a helmet of stainless steel. He was a monochrome; even his face was gray. Bar del Grillo seemed a name suitable for the place because of the slightly ambiguous meaning of *grillo* or *grilletto,* a playful and endearing name for clitoris. Many years later, in New York, I had an illumination: it was Bar and Grill."

I asked Steinberg if he remembered the names of the four sisters.

"The Cavazza sisters: in order of age, Angela Natalina, Maria, and Carla. I had to think to remember the oldest, and yet, because of her diabolical look, her name was a perfect mnemonic. She was the tallest and fattest, and, as often happens, had thin legs. (In Africa I had seen a giant antelope, the eland, which is so heavy that one hears its ankles squeaking when it moves.) She resembled Chaplin's villain—thick black eyebrows, a strong aquiline nose, flashing eyes, chin of a condottiere. Her anatomy was a mystery: her body seemed an accumulation of objects. Natalina was similar but thin, a true old maid; but she had a peasant kindness and showed compassion for me in my difficult moments. She and Carla were the feminine of the quartet. Angela and Natalina were always dressed in black. The oldest was at the cash desk and checked on everything at the only door. Carla and Natalina kept an eye on the café on the sidewalk of Via Pascoli, the billiards, the *chambres de passe,* and, in summer, the dance floor. Maria was in the kitchen, and through the little window checked on the restaurant. It was she who came out with the siphon to spray the rowdy. Among them was Bonturo, a former student at the Polytechnic. He had named himself from a verse of Dante: 'Every man there is a barrator, all but Bonturo.' Thin, with large teeth, he was one of the very few entertaining people, a big eater and hero of the brothels."

II

London. Cigar smoke. English rules of eating. The Linguists' Club. Mr. James's dictation. Maryse. A bed a hundred kilometers wide. The rod as part of the educational system.

I was late. I had stopped at a pub that was full of people with glasses in hand, as at a cocktail party, and already decorated for Christmas with lights and branches of fir. The ceiling, with beams of dark wood, had become a kind of starry sky, faded by the smoke from cigars, whose authoritative odor evoked, as always, the comfort, the security, the wealth that I will never have.

People drank with little sips, slowly. To eat and drink slowly is a rule in England, to eat very slowly, even sometimes only to pretend to eat, to be immobilized with a mouthful halfway between plate and mouth.

This position can last for a long time. You do not eat while talking, and you do not eat while someone is talking to you. When you answer, the rule is to slowly lower the fork until the mouthful has been brought back to the plate.

I crossed the entrance hall of the club to get to the cloakroom. In the view I had while taking off my overcoat, the secretary, sitting at her desk, was doing nothing; she looked to the right, offscreen, where certainly the director was, who certainly was doing nothing. The result was absolute silence, in which one heard the

crackle of the coal burning in the drawing-room fireplace; in front of the fire I saw only the older of the
Zabihi brothers, who was reading in a notebook covered with Iranian writing.

On the second floor, as I passed the women's cloakroom, the first coat, the one belonging to Mahin, was
so close to the door that I could smell its perfume; then
came Maria Asunción's gray one, with the long Scottish
scarf, Patricia's big white one, and finally the green coat
with the fur collar, above which Maryse's made-up face
was missing and, below it, her legs, which often, during dictation, made me miss words, because, looking
at the knees or the foot that she swung under the table
or slid out of her moccasin, I no longer heard, for a
moment, the voice of the professor, as if I had suddenly
become as deaf as a post. As soon as the lesson was
over, Maryse would put on her green coat in a flash
and carry her beautiful legs rapidly home. She took
them away despite our protests. She lived near the club.

⤸

There was a general sigh of relief and the sound of the
Biros set down on the table, the last Maryse's.

Mr. James, the professor, raised his eyes from the

paper that he had pulled from his wallet a few minutes earlier in front of the inquisitive faces of the students, who had come to the Linguists' Club from all over the world to learn English, an indispensable language, as the father of the Zabihi brothers would say in Teheran. Between the two brothers was thirty years' difference in age, because in Iran husbands who have the means can take up to four new wives as the first ones get old.

The older of the brothers was tall; his hair was almost white and he had a big nose, with which he would have been able to smell, by himself, all the roses of Shiraz. The younger, Morteza, was very different, but the two had in common a kind of dark shadow suffusing their eyes, their skin, their hair. Iranians, in addition to everything else, had to learn to write from left to right, as we do normally. Every so often, Morteza's hand interrupted itself as it was writing the dictation from left to right to take a quick note in Iranian, from right to left.

Maryse turned toward me.

She had a lovely face, oval, pale, sweet, and malicious. Only after a while did I realize that she had two little scars, on her chin and forehead—perhaps from an automobile accident, a horrible collision in which at first, seeing that pretty face all bloodied, they must have thought it was ruined forever. But then little by little everything clears up—I had been looking at her for several days and had remarked nothing.

"Now," said Mr. James, "I will read the dictation once more before taking it away. Come in!" he added, in the direction of the door, because someone had knocked.

The old secretary entered.

"Excuse me," she said, supporting herself with the help of a cane. "I must advise you that the day after tomorrow a visit to a big brewery will take place, leaving from here at nine A.M."

"Terrible stink," someone said under his breath.

"We do not doubt that you will be very interested in this visit. You can sign up in my office."

Maryse again turned toward me.

She had, as I said, a little scar on her chin and another on her forehead. On her forehead a tiny equilateral triangle appeared to be drawn rather than carved into the bone near the temple, but fortunately where the bone is still hard, and in fact it had withstood the blow. If Maryse had been in a slightly different position, she would have been struck on her temple—that temple, now veiled with blond hair, whose weakness made it so attractive, also, perhaps, to blows.

The scar on the chin was an irregular bit of smoother skin, a kind of wild ornament, who knows how smooth it would be . . . kissing it. I was unable to take my eyes off that mark. The space between the little scar and the mouth seemed to me an immense plain.

☙

Mrs. Grace Thompson, by profession a writer of biographies—a typically English profession—whose guest I was in her London house on Fellows Road, had the kindness to invite me to see the cottage she had outside London, in Sussex, in the village of Four Oaks—not to be confused with Five Oaks or Sevenoaks, villages in the neighborhood. It was a very small wooden structure, the ceilings little more than two meters high, the doors so low you had to stoop to go through them. There was, of course, a fireplace, in which she lighted a little fire with wood chips and sticks picked up here and there, even inside the cottage. She found a pot and put it on the fire with a little water in it, salt, and some dark seeds; and when the water boiled she took a piece of a pig's head that she had brought from London and threw it in the pot; then she went out into the tiny kitchen garden, where, despite the advanced season, some tall stalks of Brussels sprouts, almost stripped, were still standing. We gathered all the sprouts that were left, many with yellow, worm-eaten leaves, which in a different situation I would have thrown away. But Mrs. Thompson cleaned them, patiently and almost greedily, with a rusty knife, and at the end threw them, too, into the pot. After half an hour, a delicious dish was served, in two unmatching soup plates: pig's head and Brussels sprouts in their broth, without any seasoning.

The secret of this dish, which ennobles English cooking, is, I believe, in those dark seeds, which, carelessly, I forgot to find out about, and the secret has now followed Mrs. Thompson to the grave.

London has eight million inhabitants. Half are women: four million. Of these four million, a million are under thirteen and two million are over twenty-five. Of the remaining let's now discard the less pretty girls and those of unpleasant disposition—let's discard, in short, nine-tenths of the million. There will remain—look what it means, a big city like London—a hundred thousand beautiful girls. If I calculate that in bed each of them takes up a meter of space, they could sleep in a bed a hundred kilometers wide, and just to kiss them all good night would take . . . or, making a date with all of them for tomorrow at noon in the usual place and assuming that each one arrives half an hour late, I would wait . . . only until half past twelve. I say "only" because you don't have to add up all the delays, as you might think at first.

When the thermometer had descended to the minimum and snowflakes came whirling into the classroom through the window—open, according to English custom—Mr. James arrived wearing a scarf. Always without coat and hat but with a sky-blue scarf that he considered a kind of weakness and immediately offered to the coldest female student. He had never had an overcoat. Many years before, he had had a hat, which he used, however, only when following a funeral, holding it in his hand, never on his head. He told us that G. B. Shaw had worn the same tweed jacket for forty years, he boasted of the usefulness of caning as part of the educational system, and he recalled the choice his teacher had allowed him between a thin cane and a thicker one. He had chosen the thinner but had then learned that the thicker hurts less. Since he was Welsh, he did not fail to hum songs and to cite as an example of the oddities of his land the name of a little town in North Wales: Llanfairpowllgwyngyllgogerychwydrobwlll-lantysiliogogogoch.

I almost forgot one oddity of the Linguists' Club: Mrs. Russ, the best professor of English at the club, looked like the Queen Mother of England; her daughter, also a professor at the club, looked like Queen Elizabeth; the daughter's husband, incredible though it may seem, looked like Prince Philip, Duke of Edinburgh—exactly like two peas in a pod.

III

The tropics. The iguana. Wilma, the youngest typist. A night in Iztapa, on the edge of the Pacific. Lichtenberg and his knife. The spinach soufflé. The fragrance of the young apprentice. The boiled beef at the restaurant of the Hotel Moskva and the young blonde's letter.

"Nemesio Xiú, the Mayan king, died two years ago here at Ticúl, in Yucatan. Nemesio had an ancient book. One day the governor of Merida called him and offered him a piece of land in exchange for the book. It seems that the book indicated where the treasure of Uxmal was hidden. But he didn't sell it, either through fear of a curse or for other reasons. It seems that some Americans made a copy of it. Xiú means grass, the prince of grass, and by grass they probably meant corn, the basis of Mayan agriculture and civilization.

"Nemesio is buried here, in the cemetery of Ticúl. Strange tombs: in particular, a villa tomb, half a meter high, with miniature windows and shutters, and a lighthouse tomb, to be seen mainly at night. In town there was the noise of the carnival, but here is the true silence of the tomb, a silence that at first almost hurts the ears. We sit on the tombs and take out *biscotellas,* marvelous toasted pieces of sponge cake, a specialty of Ticúl. And after the *biscotellas,* which are delicious but dry, a swallow of rum, Bacardi *carta blanca,* to the health of the ———. The shutters of the villa tomb are movable, so the ——— can, if he wants, open them or keep them closed, as he does now, given the intense heat, though the sun is setting.

"In front of the inn there were already some cars, dripping with the nighttime humidity. Going out, I found my feet sinking into sand, and as soon as the door slammed I heard the roar of the waves breaking a hundred meters away.

"On the ground behind the entrance the porter slept, half naked, under a low mosquito net. He awoke, came out from under the net, pushed aside the coverlet on which he had been sleeping, opened the door, brought in the suitcases, collected the documents, took the keys, picked up the suitcases. He seemed a sleepwalker.

"We went out into an open courtyard with tall weeds. Inside and outside the heat was always the same. A big iguana in the grass woke up and, running crazily, fled, with a sudden, horrible rustling."

"How disgusting!" said Wilma. "I wouldn't go there, to those places, not even if you paid me!" Wilma was the youngest; she took seriously everything that was dictated to her. Like all the girls at the typing agency, she was fat—her agility was concentrated in her hands. Her black smock, which was tight and short, forced her to a continuous effort of rearrangement.

"The iguana," I said, "is a big harmless lizard; in fact it's useful, because it eats flies and cockroaches, like a toad. . . . I remember a night in Iztapa, in Guatemala, on the shore of the Pacific. The moon rose like an immense red disk. It was the hour in which authoresses dip their pens in the inkwell and the howler monkeys, moving in herds through the treetops, roar like lions.

The motorboat crossed the lagoon and landed on the sand spit that separates the lagoon from the ocean, in front of the Ranchito Michatoya, where I was living. The motionless water of the lagoon seemed to reflect the clearer sky of an hour before, still a little violet; it was tardy in comparison with the ocean, which was already black, like the profundity of night.

"Before going to bed I'd take a walk on the beach, which was scattered with Indians, who slept in the open to save money on lodging, and with the fires of braziers for making coffee. The moon had become orange; it was so enormous it could not detach itself from the horizon.

"At the Ranchito Michatoya—as at the two others, the Michoyan and the Brisas del Pacifico—the walls of the rooms were of loosely braided matting: I mean you could easily see through it. While I was in bed, in the dark, I saw a candle enter the next room. It was a young Indian girl with a long black braid. She set the candle on a chair and began to unbraid her hair."

"Let's go on writing," said Wilma, pulling her smock down over her legs.

"Okay," I said. "We entered a corridor; the floor was bathed in oil and sparkled in the faint light. The porter walked rapidly, kicking the slower cockroaches with his bare feet. Opened the door of my room, turned on the light, put the suitcase on the stool, and disappeared without waiting for a tip, perhaps for fear of hearing demands or complaints, or perhaps because he was in a hurry to go back to sleep.

"The chest of drawers was of heavy mahogany. I opened a drawer; there was a cockroach. At the window, the metallic mosquito netting had holes in it. Illuminated by the moon, the phosphorescent crests of the long ocean waves rose continuously out of the darkness, coming forward toward the inn. It was best to hurry. I put my stuff on top of the closed suitcase, sat down on the bed, looked around at the floor, the walls, and the ceiling, pulled down the mosquito net, and turned out the light.

"The roar of the waves was loud, and so was the croaking of the frogs. The smell of oil was mixed with the nauseating scent of the poison sprayed against mosquitoes, which were almost certainly entering, one after the other, through the holes in the net. I seemed to hear a rustling, the horrible rustling of the iguana. . . .

"Next morning, with the sun, cockroaches iguana

mosquitoes and frogs had disappeared, who knows where. The porter was behind the counter, talking to the customers like a normal porter at an inn. On the beach a fresh breeze arrived from offshore with the waves; the water was warm."

"There," said Wilma, stopping her typing for a moment. "That's where I'd like to go."

☙

Lichtenberg wrote of a man who "was working on a system of natural history in which he had classified the animals according to the shape of their excrement." He singled out three categories: cylindrical, spherical, and cake-shaped. "Where he jokes," Goethe said of him, "there a problem lies hidden."

Georg Christoph Lichtenberg was a German writer of the eighteenth century. He was a hunchback. At thirty-five he fell in love with a girl of twelve, and he lived with her until she died, five years later. He was the inventor of an object that became famous, nearly as famous as Galileo's pendulum or Newton's apple or Möbius's strip: the knife that has no blade and whose handle is missing.

When I was a high school student, my old philoso-

phy professor often cited Lichtenberg's knife and
smiled. He smiled on his own account, because the students were too young to appreciate this wonderful invention: it seemed a joke that wasn't funny, and they
laughed at the professor's smile. To understand something it is necessary to have lived a long time, perhaps
to die . . . and to live again. A dead man coming out
of the tomb would be the best master of life. Seated on
his own name incised in the granite slab as shiny as a
mirror, and turned toward the sun that has warmed the
stone—now, finally, he understands the value of a ray
of sun, and he could, I believe, make us understand it.

☞

While I was eating, I thought of being the blind man
who sits on the sidewalk under the elevated tracks,
waiting only for that fragrance to pass before me, with
my good wolf dog beside me all day, a little plastic pail
in his mouth, looking passersby in the eye, one by one,
to induce them to give alms. The pail has a cover with
a funnel that lets money go in but keeps the dishonest
from stealing while they pretend to give something.
Unless the blind man is a fake blind man who thought
of the funnel as a way of giving an air of authenticity to

his disguise. The man who sells eggs a little beyond the blind man had a deal for housewives: a little suitcase full of broken eggs, at a reduced price. His head, oval and balding, with insignificant features, resembled an egg more and more every day. Meanwhile, the first drops of a storm were coming down. The blind man, his dog, and the egg man were in the shelter of the elevated; the girl, afraid of getting wet, had begun to run. It was no longer I who was thinking, my brain was running on its own, I could not even manage to keep up with it. . . . Only when the servant put down on my left the plate with the spinach soufflé did I forget for a moment that fragrance and return to see everything, as if waking from a dream: the host, his diamond rings, his mother, who had cooked the spinach soufflé herself, the splendid, lavishly set table, the English, Russian, and Oriental silver, the precious Persian carpets.

"My son is a little mad," said the mother. "At night he gets up and counts his seventy carpets to see if they're all there, he calls them by name. . . . Take a good helping!"

The soufflé, presented on a marvelous round plate, was cut into wedges and covered with a light tomato sauce. For serving yourself, there was a silver trowel, like the one used by the Pope to wall up the door of the Holy Year. When I came across the young apprentice perfumer, she was running toward the bar to get a coffee for her boss. For a second she was thirty centimeters away, on my left, like the spinach soufflé.

"A little more," the mother insisted.

I pushed the trowel under another piece, the air moved by her passage hit me in the face, I smelled the perfume of the perfume shop, sum of all perfumes, together with the particular, personal fragrance of the young apprentice, which vaguely resembled the fresh scent of certain deodorants, a fragrance that only certain girls have, a family of girls, or a special race, and whose basic characteristics I don't know how to indicate, because when I happen to smell it, emotion keeps me from taking notes. The trowel was on the point of falling from my hand and, perhaps, hitting the precious plate, breaking it and staining the tablecloth and the carpet with tomato sauce. I turned to look at the soufflé, also behind it.

⬚

Coffee was served in the drawing room, among hundreds of precious silver knickknacks, placed here and there, wherever there was a shelf or a console table, on which the mother, before sinking definitively into the armchair with her cup of coffee, had thrown an automatic and unsympathetic look of inspection.

The strangest knickknack was a kind of silver egg, perforated all over, that opened on a hinge, like a hard-boiled egg cut in half for a salad: an ancient Yugoslav soap dish for traveling. The traveler, a typical Yugoslav— that is, a man tall or short, fat or thin, blond or very dark, yet immediately recognizable as a Yugoslav— had disembarked at the Moskva Hotel, built of yellow stone and decorated by the snow that lingered on its cornices and by stripes of green majolica tile; and in spite of the inviting waves of Gypsy music and the familiar odor of onions and *rakija* arriving from the restaurant through the revolving door, he went directly up to his room to wash his hands.

When we had finished our coffee, the host took off the three diamond rings whose bluish brilliance had pleasantly reminded him, during dinner, that he was free of the horror of poverty, and went off to his bedroom for his *pennichella,* the afternoon nap that Romans cannot do without.

But the ancient Yugoslav traveler, who was slowly taking shape, was now sitting at a table in the restaurant of the Moskva Hotel before an oval plate on which there was a generous helping of exquisite boiled beef with horseradish sauce. The salt was missing. The traveler put his knife down on the tablecloth, which was more spotted than a leopard's skin, and made a sign to the approaching waiter.

The waiter, instead of stopping, passed by and continued on toward a table where no one had called him, and began to remove the crumbs from the tablecloth with a napkin, working fanatically, roughly pushing aside the diners, moving their arms violently, on the pretext that beneath them were some crumbs. From other tables, other customers without salt or paprika or napkins nodded or called to him.

In this situation charged with electricity, the merest trifle would have been enough. . . . But nothing happened.

Or, rather: a blond young woman, coming from the powder room, gracefully swaying on her high heels, crossed the room directly to the center, where, under the glass roof and around the gushing fountain, the most visible tables were. Sitting alone at one of these tables, she gazed at the traveler for a long time, with a penetrating sweetness, as if, with her eyes, she were writing him a letter. At this point, with a smile of triumph, the waiter put a salt cellar down on the traveler's table. The traveler took a pinch of salt, scattered it carefully over his beef, then cut a good-sized piece, both fat and lean, covered it with horseradish sauce, and, bending his face over his plate, brought it to his mouth.

The blonde interrupted the letter. She took a Drina out of her cigarette case and, changing the direction of her glance, lighted it with the gesture of a grande dame.

IV

Be a cook? The rest home. Switzerland. The creation of the world. Via San Giovanni di Dio. A touching object. The train stops.

My dear friend, I'm afraid I will be forever poor, which is a terrible thing, given that pleasures cost more and more. I saw our friend, who was taking the sun on the edge of the pool. I found him grown old in his feet. But let's ignore the details. I bring to your attention: Thomas Browne (1605–82), "Hydriotaphia, or Urn Burial," a treatise on the ancient uses of cremation and the gathering of the ashes in funerary urns, which you will find easily at the nearest newsstand. Yesterday I did nothing. I am tired of swimming and always finding myself in the open sea! Send them all to hell! That is, let them stay here! The book "Graves," etc., arouses mistrust because of its theme, as I foresaw. I am training hard for the bad news, changing careers, frugality . . .

Be a cook? I've also thought of that, but I'm sure I would be too intolerant. If a customer should say to me that the steak is badly cooked I would immediately murder him. These are things that it's better only to think about, to avoid the boredom of what would follow: trial, summations by prosecution and defense, life imprisonment . . .

The rest home is not far from the border, and the attendants all have an obsession with contraband. The door to the terrace was obstructed by a group of old patients who wanted to reenter and were being ceremonious about precedence; their movements were so slow that, with all their efforts, they practically stood still. Beyond the balustrade stretched Switzerland, with its calm, its security, order, tranquillity. Down below, in the garden, were two pheasants in a big cage, and just below—that is, on the path under the balustrade—were the rinds of oranges and the wrappers of candies brought by visitors on Sunday. A latecomer was climbing the staircase, grasping the railing with both hands. After every step he stopped for a few minutes to catch his breath. In half an hour, an hour at the most, even he would be at the top. I took out a piece of candy. Well . . .

Well, God created Heaven and Earth first. The candy was of alpine herbs, never mind. Then the animals: those that fly, those that live in water, and those that live on land. The mosquito looked for man to nourish itself on his blood, and didn't find him. God was very busy. He didn't have a moment to spare. Oddly, given his nature, he felt the need for a day of rest. Only at the end of the week did he find time to provide for the mosquito. I put the candy in my mouth and threw away the wrapper, down into Via San Giovanni di Dio, where grass is growing because usually no one passes that way. It's a path, not more than fifty meters long, where the previous Sunday I had come across a touching object in the form of a cake, according to Lichtenberg's classification: cattle dung—that is, cow excrement, a cow pie.

I wake because of the sudden silence. The train has stopped at an unknown station. With a thousand useless gestures, the grandfather prepares the meal for the fidgety grandchild, who, held by the grandmother, is standing at the window. Thermos, sugar, napkin, cup continually change places.

Grandfather: Stay still, where do you want to go? Don't you see it's dark outside? Outside is the wolf . . . who will eat you. If you fall, there's no doctor here in the station.

Grandson: There's no doctor?

Grandfather: No, there isn't.

Grandson: And ambulance?

Grandfather: No ambulance. If you fall, you'll die.

Grandson: And then?

Grandfather: And then you're dead.

Grandson: And then?

Grandfather: And then you go to the cemetery.

Grandson: And then?

Grandmother (tenderly embracing the boy): And then they put you underground.

V

The moment to conclude. Pliny the Elder and Pliny the Younger. The degree in architecture. Landru's last meal. Again the beautiful waitress of Crescenzago. Eve's navel. The new generation.

The moment to conclude had arrived.

"I was born here in Como," I said, "in the city of Pliny the Elder and Pliny the Younger. The Elder (Gaius Plinius the Second) is the author of the endless *Natural History,* and Como dedicated to him the street that runs from Piazza Cavour, where the port once was, to Piazza del Duomo: a neoclassical street that is absolutely straight, perhaps too straight. Le Corbusier said that straight streets are drawn by man, while crooked ones were drawn by asses. But in this preference for straight streets and everything rectilinear the Swiss architect was perhaps mistaken. Pliny the Younger (nephew of the Elder) was a rather boring litterateur. He had two villas on the lake. He called the first Comedy, the second Tragedy. (Here is the litterateur.) He loved the lake of Como because, he wrote, on its banks one could study, fish, and hunt at the same time. (Again literature.) But he nevertheless had a right to be recognized by his fellow citizens, to whom he had given a library, to encourage them to read. And once he offered to all the citizenry a banquet—whose menu, however, he forgot to transcribe in his letters. When Proust was asked who he would have liked to be if he had not been Proust he replied: 'Pliny the Younger.' But he was only fourteen.

"I was born here in August, under the sign of the Lion. (If the two Plinys were alive today, they would both be around two thousand years old, and it would be difficult to distinguish the Elder from the Younger.) Under this sign, says Trimalcio, gluttons (*cataphagae*) are born; perhaps my surname, Buzzi, derives from *buzzo* (stomach). But apart from the fact that Trimalcio's ramblings are unreliable, Buzzi derives from the Latin Albutii. There is in Rome (it seems) an ancient marble stele in which the name Albutius is carved, along with the emblems of a mason: plumb line, a Roman foot measure, a square. A Buzzi (it seems) worked on the duomo of Orvieto; and the architect Carlo Buzzi is mentioned in connection with the façade of the duomo of Milan, in the sixteen hundreds. Thus, following a hypothetical family tradition, I got my degree in architecture. Architecture, like music, refines one's manners. Even a monster like Henri Desiré Landru owes to the fact that he worked as a draftsman in an architectural firm the refinement he demonstrated in the choice of the menu for his last meal, in his prison cell at Versailles, the evening of February 24, 1922: cold chicken, fried potatoes, mineral water, coffee—a pack lunch for traveling. We animals, Linnaeus, the successor to our dear old Pliny, says, approximately, we grow, we live, and we feel: '*Lapides crescunt; vegetabilia crescunt et vivunt; animalia crescunt, vivunt et sentiunt.*' Living and feeling distinguish us from the minerals, while only feeling distinguishes us from a turnip or a beet."

The car of the funicular looked like a fly, and the former annex of the Hotel Milano, up at Brunate, like a box of Swedish matches. The cruel spring sun made minerals, vegetables, and animals sparkle.

"That's all," I added.

☞

"Isn't there still that little restaurant in Crescenzago?"

The sudden question was followed by a silence that became more and more embarrassing as it was prolonged. To give an answer was for me more difficult than to hammer a nail with a banana, as Americans say, or, as Monselet says, "to establish precise rules for making a bouquet garni." But I could not stay silent forever, as I would have liked to.

"You must know," I said, "that in America the birds don't sing; rather, they make noises as if they were tropical birds. In America the nightingale doesn't exist, and no one has ever thought of importing it from Europe. Also keep in mind that in the earthly paradise—the Garden of Eden—Adam's happiness lacked only the navel of Eve, who, not being born of woman, like Adam, did not have one—a detail that many painters and sculptors have forgotten. I will say more: for a Turk or an Egyptian—that is, for anyone fanatical about belly dancing—Eve would be lacking something essential; but even for one of the unfaithful, a female belly without the navel would be a terrible disappointment, like a Frau armchair without the *capitonné*."

From inside the bar came the sound of billiards. Two young men were having a game. They had put on professional smocks to protect the material of their pants. Behind the bar, the girl was washing unbreakable cups and glasses with her beautiful hands. Another new generation was succeeding the previous one, waiting—this one, too—to disappear into nothing, like the chapel of San Carlo Borromeo that stood in the square in Gorgonzola.

Notes

4 "before planting itself": Anton Chekhov, "A Nightmare."

4 "ninety proof, not eighty": Mikhail Bulgakov, *Heart of a Dog.*

5 "vodka of Koshelyov": Chekhov, "The Duel."

5 "looked at me obliquely": Chekhov, *The Island of Sakhalin.*

5 "Better a tomtit": Nikolai Gogol, *Dead Souls.*

6 "It is a mixture": Joseph Roth, *Reise in Russland* [*Viaggio in Russia*].

7 "where even the butterflies sting": Viktor Shklovsky, *Gamburgskii Schet* [*Il Punteggio di Amburgo*].

7 Leonid Abalkin, Academy of Sciences: *Les Nouvelles de Moscou,* June 21, 1987.

8 "The prisoners": Chekhov, *The Island of Sakhalin.*

9 "He showed me his buttocks": Ibid.

9 "At night when you enter": Chekhov, Letter to Maria Chekhova, May 14–17, 1890.

10 "As everyone knows": Ivan Turgenev, *Fathers and Sons*.

11 "And you who, through work": Vladimir Mayakovsky, "A Few Words in Favor of Certain Vices."

12 "What a sauté": Leo Tolstoy, *War and Peace*.

13 "calling them Tartars": Giampaolo Dossena, *Storia Confidenziale della Letteratura Italiana. Dalle Origini a Dante*. Milano, 1987.

13 "An uninvited guest": Chekhov, *Platonov*.

13 "Traveling": Osip Mandelstam, *Journey to Armenia*.

15 Cossack names: Gogol, *Taras Bulba*.

15 Cossack war cry: Henri Troyat, *Daily Life in Russia Under the Last Czar*.

15 "Crows, numberless as flies": Gogol, *Dead Souls*.

15 "For the third day": Arsenii Tarkovsky, "A Day in Winter."

16 "the most respectable bird": Turgenev, *Fathers and Sons*.

17 "In Russia everything loves": Gogol, *Dead Souls*.

17 the Bobolina: Ibid.

17 "Russia of the heavy buttocks": Alexander Blok, "The Twelve (Bolshevik Songs)."

17 "I love their little feet": Alexander Pushkin, *Eugene Onegin.*

18 Tolstoy's pillow: Tatiana Tolstaya, *Tolstoy Remembered.*

18 amputee: Mandelstam, *Journey to Armenia.*

18 a common custom: Fyodor Dostoyevsky, *The Diary of a Writer.*

19 "Russian tendency to spend": Chekhov, *The Island of Sakhalin.*

19 Auden: in Joseph Brodsky, "Less Than One," in *Selected Essays.*

20 "that is, the cemetery": Chekhov, Letter to Maria Chekhova, September 22, 1894.

20 "In the villages": Chekhov, *The Island of Sakhalin.*

20 "During the night": Chekhov, Letter to Maria Chekhova, April 25, 1887.

21 "At night it is a true martyrdom": Chekhov, Letters to Maria Chekhova, April 7–10 and 17–19, 1887.

21 "Yakov Andreyich resembled": Chekhov, Letter to Maria Chekhova, April 7–10, 1887.

21   "What a son": Turgenev, "Notes of a Hunter."

22   The Russians called trousers: Chekhov, "In a Hotel."

22   hemorrhoids: Chekhov, *The Island of Sakhalin.*

23   "weakness": Chekhov, "Terror."

24   "where the trams": Shklovsky, *Khod Konya [La Mossa del Cavallo].*

24   "Good vodka!": Chekhov, *Three Sisters.*

24   Gorilka: Chekhov, Letter to Aleksei S. Suvorin, August 7, 1895.

25   "An olivelike color": Gogol, *Dead Souls.*

26   "Beside his book": Chekhov, "Ward No. 6."

26   "I don't like their cooking": Louis-Ferdinand Céline, *Trifles for a Massacre.*

27   "a gigantic watermelon": Gogol, *Dead Souls.*

27   "an immense heap": Céline, *Trifles for a Massacre.*

27   Escoffier: Auguste Escoffier, *Souvenirs Inédits,* Marseilles, 1985.

28   "On his beard": Chekhov, "The Kingdom of Women."

28   "What I desire": Pushkin, *Eugene Onegin.*

28   "smoker of the sky": Gogol, *Dead Souls.*

28   "What shall we eat?": Tolstoy, *Resurrection.*

29   Ukrainian borscht: Chekhov, "The Man in a Case."

29 Zilin: Chekhov, "The Siren's Song."

30 "Our peasant blows": Chekhov, "Ariadne."

30 *limonade de cochon:* Tolstoy, *War and Peace.*

30 "a murmuring": Chekhov, *The Island of Sakhalin.*

31 Chekhov's letters to his wife: Nov. 8, 1903; March 6, 1904; Sept. 9, 1904; Nov. 21, 1903; March 29, 1904; Oct. 21, 1903; March 6, 1904; March 29, 1904; March 18, 1904; Jan. 13, 1903; Oct. 29, 1901; Feb. 6, 1902.

31 "city of Tartars": Chekhov, Letter to Aleksei N. Pleshcheev, Aug. 3, 1889.

32 "A house with four rooms": Chekhov, Letter to Maria Chekhova, Dec. 8, 1898.

32 "My dream": Chekhov, Letter to Aleksei S. Suvorin, Aug. 24, 1893.

33 "O sister bitches": Sergei Esenin, "Le Nave delle Cavalle."

33 "Over there": Céline, *Mea Culpa.*

33 "Man needs everything": Mikhail Saltykov Shchedrin, *The Golovlyov Family.*

33 "He gave me some water": Nikolai Leskov, *The Enchanted Pilgrim.*

33 "In the event of inhaling": Ivan Goncharov, *Oblomov.*

34 "You are very pretty": Chekhov, "Three Years."

35 Kremlin of Gadda: Carlo Emilio Gadda, *Le Meraviglie d'Italia*, Turin, 1964.

36 "like horses being put in harness": Goncharov, *Oblomov*.

36 "arch-bully": Vladimir Nabokov, *Speak, Memory*.

37 "He had patches": Marina Svetayeva, "Lines for Pushkin."

37 "When his bier was opened": Roth, *Reise in Russland*.

38 "I believe I am the only person": Antonio Delfini, *Diari 1927–1961*.

39 Panshin: Turgenev, *Home of the Gentry*.

40 "sultriness, dust": Dostoyevsky, *The Diary of a Writer*.

40 spire of the Admirality: Chekhov, "The Album."

41 the barber Ivan Yakovlevich: Gogol, "The Nose."

42 "But here a thick fog": Ibid.

42 a house "whose population": Goncharov, *Oblomov*.

42 "I have never put on stockings by myself": Ibid.

42 "The aim of my life": Curzio Suckert Malaparte, *Lenin Buonanima*, Firenze, 1962.

42 "incapable of doing anything": Leon Trotsky, *History of the Russian Revolution*.

43 a begging dog: Shklovsky, *La Mossa del Cavallo.*

43 "a noted poet": Chekhov, *The Island of Sakhalin.*

44 "I learned the alphabet": Mayakovsky, "I Love (My University)."

45 "with their enormous behinds": Tolstoy, *Resurrection.*

45 "There must be great mansions": Chekhov, *On the High Road.*

45 "All coachmen": Dostoyevsky, *The House of the Dead.*

46 "The poor in general": In Emilio Radius, *Verdi Vivo,* Milan, 1951.

46 Timofey: Troyat, *Tolstoy.*

47 Verdi's meal: Giovanni Cenzato, *Itinerari Verdiani.*

48 Frate Indovino: *La Buona Cucina Casalinga—1000 Ricette di Frate Indovino.* Perugia, 1968.

48 Thieves were thrown: Shklovsky, *Sentimental Journey.*

49 "among raccoon coats": Goncharov, *Oblomov.*

49 "There is nothing more beautiful": Gogol, "The Prospect."

49 "The broad, tedious street": Dostoyevsky, *The Diary of a Writer.*

49   "the main artery": Leon Trotsky, *History of the Russian Revolution.*

49   "From 1836": Gogol, "Petersburg 1836."

50   "Esenin says something": Mikhail Zoshchenko, *Before the Sunrise.*

50   "Better in fact": Mayakovsky, "Sergei Esenin."

51   "latrine cleaner": Mayakovsky, "At the Top of My Voice—First Prelude to the Poem."

51   "he is the driver": Svetayeva, "To Vladimir Mayakovsky."

52   "I do not want to lie": Anna Grigorievna Dostoyevsky, *Dostoyevsky Portrayed by His Wife.*

53   "murderous slumber": William Shakespeare, *Julius Caesar.*

54   "Their beards": Tolstoy, *Letters of Tolstoy and His Cousin Aleksandra Andreyevna Tolstaya.*

54   "No Russian writer": André Gide, *Return from the U.S.S.R.*

54   "*The Mother* is": Troyat, *Tolstoy.*

54   "I read the end": Chekhov, Letter to Olga Knipper, Dec. 7, 1901.

54   "Another piece of advice": Chekhov, Letter to Aleksei Peshkov (Gorky), Sept. 3, 1899.

57 the parasite—"whom Russian literature": Tolstoy, *The Decembrists.*

57 "Gentlemen of easy temper": Dostoyevsky, *The Brothers Karamazov.*

58 "the apotheosis of drunkenness": Dostoyevsky, *The Village of Stepanchikovo and Its Inhabitants.*

59 "I have absolutely no idea": Anna Grigorievna Dostoyevsky, *Dostoyevsky Portrayed by His Wife.*

59 "under the whip": Ibid.

59 *Poor Folk:* Dostoyevsky, *The Diary of a Writer.*

60 "teeth were like pearls": Dostoyevsky, *The Possessed.*

60 Levin: Dostoyevsky, *The Diary of a Writer.*

60 He loved eel . . . talk to the coachman: Anna Grigorievna Dostoyevsky, *Dostoyevsky Portrayed by His Wife.*

60 "Or is it possible": Dostoyevsky, *Notes from Underground.*

60 Flaiano: Ennio Flaiano, *Un Bel Giorno di Libertà,* Milano, 1979.

60 Count Aleksei Tolstoy: Slonim, *Soviet Russian Literature.*

62 "sighs of Nikolai": Troyat, *Tolstoy.*

62   Ella Wheeler Wilcox: Nabokov, *Speak, Memory.*

63   Death of Chekhov: The touching description of
     Chekhov's end—reported by two of his biogra-
     phers, Natalia Ginzburg (*Vita Attraverso le Lettere,*
     Torino, 1989) and Troyat (*Chekhov*), neither of
     whom provides notes on its origin—should
     surely be attributed to Olga Knipper, the beloved
     cockroach, who was the only witness, aside from
     Dr. Schworer, of that death.

JOURNEY TO THE LAND OF THE FLIES

69   impudence of the fly: Serafino Amabile Guastella,
     Le Parità e le Storie Morali dei Nostri Villani, Milano,
     1976.

69   St. Bartholomew: Nabokov, *Pnin.*

TRAVELS TO DJAKARTA, GORGONZOLA, CRESCENZAGO, LONDON, MILAN

99   "As a young man": André Gide, *Journal
     1889–1913.*

99   "Handsome as a dissertation": Comte de
     Lautréamont, *Maldoror.*

100   "It's no longer horsemeat": Victor Hugo, *Things Seen.*

103   "If he has turbot": Ibid.

104   "Zeno, as the founder": Giuseppe Averani, *Del Vitto e delle Cene degli Antichi,* Milano, 1863.

FIRST TRAVELS

105   "One eye": Heinrich Heine, *Autobiography.*

106   the Athenians, "having dined": Herodotus, *Histories.*

107   Countess Hahn-Hahn: Richard Wagner, *My Life.*

122   a man "who was working": Georg Christoph Lichtenberg, *Schriften und Briefe.*

132   Pliny the Younger: Pliny the Younger, *Letters.*

134   "*Lapides crescunt*": Carl von Linné, *Systema Naturae.*

134   "bouquet garni": Charles Monselet, *Lettres Gourmandes,* Paris, 1877.

ALDO BUZZI trained as an architect in Milan, where he now lives. He worked in the Italian cinema for many years and then as a publisher. His writing has appeared in many literary journals and he has had several books published in Italy. This book was originally published by Mondadori under the title *Chekhov a Sondrio e Altri Viaggi*.

A BOUT THE TYPE

This book was set in Perpetua, a typeface designed by the English artist Eric Gill, and cut by The Monotype Corporation between 1928 and 1930. Perpetua is a contemporary face of original design, without any direct historical antecedents. The shapes of the roman letters are derived from the techniques of stonecutting. The larger display sizes are extremely elegant and form a most distinguished series of inscriptional letters.